ADOPTION CRISIS

ADOPTION CRISIS

The Truth behind Adoption and Foster Care

Carole A. McKelvey
and
Dr. JoEllen Stevens

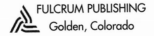

FULCRUM PUBLISHING
Golden, Colorado

Copyright © 1994 Carole A. McKelvey and Dr. JoEllen Stevens

The authors assume full responsibility for the details and assertions of each account and have taken every measure to preserve the anonymity of the subjects and case histories contained herein. Names have often been changed to protect individuals. All quoted material is taken from actual case histories, interviews or cited sources.

Library of Congress Cataloging-in-Publication Data

McKelvey, Carole A.
    The adoption crisis : the truth behind adoption and foster care / Carole A. McKelvey and JoEllen Stevens.
        p.   cm.
    Includes bibliographical references and index.
    ISBN 1-55591-172-2
    1. Adoption—United States. 2. Foster home care—United States.
I. Stevens, JoEllen. II. Title.
HV875.55.M37   1994
362.7'33'0973—dc20   93–51055
                                                          CIP

Printed in the United States of America
0 9 8 7 6 5 4 3 2 1

Fulcrum Publishing
350 Indiana Street, Suite 350
Golden, Colorado 80401-5093

*To all the little ones in America
who are searching to find their way home*

TABLE OF CONTENTS

CONCLUSIONS

APPENDICES

FOREWORD

Each year in America, more than a million potential parents set out on a singular goal—to adopt a child. For many aging baby boomers, time has run out on their biological clocks. For others, infertility has made the dream of children impossible. Adoption has become their only hope.

I am an adoptive parent. I have personally found the adoptive process to be filled with grace and integrity, which only confirmed my sincere belief that children choose their parents and are ultimately responsible for the circumstances of their lives. Unfortunately, this is not always the case.

Today many legal and ethical dilemmas have invaded the adoption world. We also see many, many children who have been hurt by the foster care system, having been moved from place to place to place with an ever-diminishing hope of finding the family they long for.

Some of these children have "special needs" which must be considered, children who are older, are members of sibling groups, are mentally or physically challenged, are members of minority groups or suffer as a result of drug-addicted or alcoholic biological parents. These children are becoming more unattached and psychologically disturbed each day as they see their childhoods slipping away in one placement after another.

All of these children have the potential to become happy, healthy and productive individuals as members of loving and caring families. In the end, they can become responsible and compassionate adults capable of making positive contributions to their world while raising happy and healthy children of their own.

In this book, you will discover the challenges of parenting an adopted child and some ways these challenges can be met. You will learn about "family fit" and how to find a child, even one with special needs, whom you can live with and love.

There are inherent difficulties in the adoption process as it now exists. Adoption workers, potential adoptive parents and, in fact, all of us must work together to be sure we do not lose one of our most important assets—the children who are our future.

Adoption should not be a promise unfulfilled. It should result in dreams that come true, as it has for me and my two adopted children, Zak and Anna Kate. The child who was born in your heart can some-day be in your arms. This book can help you find your way to each other.

Peace!
John Denver

ACKNOWLEDGMENTS

This book is the result of the first collaboration of Carole A. McKelvey and her sister, Dr. JoEllen Stevens, Ph.D. At first, the authors worried about how the work might affect their relationship as sisters. We shouldn't have. It was a gratifying experience that brought us even closer together.

There are a great number of people to whom we are grateful for making this work possible and fruitful!

It is a book we felt must be written because of the pain so many families with adopted children expressed to Carole McKelvey after her first book was published. *High Risk: Children without a Conscience* was written with Ken Magid, Ph.D., in 1988 and published by Bantam Books. Only after hearing their frustrations, disappointments and triumphs did we fully understand the dynamics operating in so many American and Canadian households.

As we worked on this book, it became clear that the child welfare system in this country is not serving the children it was set up to help. We found ourselves repeating the question: Who speaks for the children? There are very few advocates for these small victims, but we found a few:

- Our friends at the nonprofit Attachment Center at Evergreen, Colorado;
- Our friends and colleagues Connell Watkins and Associates of Evergreen, Colorado;
- Dr. Foster Cline, also of Evergreen; and
- Dixie van de Flier Davis of the Rocky Mountain Adoption Exchange.

We also want to acknowledge the help of parents Gail Trenberth, Debbe Magnusen, Dianna Lynn and Robert White, Kimm and Greg Bolding, Art and Jenny Scovis, Ilona and Toby Scott and Peter Forsythe of the Edna McConnell Clark Foundation. We can not leave out the knowledgeable people who run the North American Council on Adoptable Children.

We also like to think that we, too, speak for the children. We speak for the future Stephanies, Angies, Beckys, Levis and Michaels. We hope the little ones who follow do not fall into the same tragic circumstances that we have divulged herein.

We are grateful for the aid and guidance of our editors at Fulcrum Publishing in Golden, Colorado, our very talented researchers Stacey Williams, Donna Spevack and Julie Anderson and artist Ian Andrew McKelvey. We also appreciate the support and friendship of Verna Noel Jones, Marlys Duran and Howard Stevens, Ph.D., whose contributions to this book were many.

Carole thanks the women who support the work of writers, artists and scholars through the Rocky Mountain Women's Institute, and her colleagues in the Journalism and Women's Symposium (JAWS). Thanks for your support and encouragement.

This book couldn't have been written without the aid and honesty of so many members of the adoption triad. They have our undying gratitude for so openly sharing their life stories. We wish them all the best.

We also thank John Denver for his belief in this project and its goals, and for writing the foreword to our book. He is a true friend of the children.

Most importantly, we thank our families for their patience and support. We couldn't have done it without George, Ian, Heather and Fawn McKelvey, and Howard, Eric, Sean and Lacey Stevens.

We must also not leave out our devotion to our mother and father, Geri and Francis Conner. Thank you for always telling us we could do anything that we put our minds to.

The authors wish to acknowledge the use of information from these sources:

The National Committee for Adoption through its book, *The Adoption Factbook*; 1930 Seventeenth St. NW, Washington, DC 20009.

The North American Council on Adoptable Children (NACAC), through its newsletter, *Adoptalk*; 1821 University Ave., Suite N-498, St. Paul, MN 55104.

The case files of the Attachment Center at Evergreen, Connell Watkins and Dr. Foster Cline.

The National Association for Perinatal Addiction, Research and Education (NAPARE) of Chicago, IL, on drug-exposed infants.

The International Concerns Committee for Children (ICCC), Boulder, CO.

All of the stories and case studies in this book are certified by the authors as being the true case histories and stories of real individuals who have consented to be interviewed. These events actually happened. Real names are used in most instances, but some have been changed to protect the individuals.

Throughout *Adoption Crisis* the authors have chosen to use only gender pronouns, for two reasons:

- Demographics—When speaking of children's care givers and the formation of attachments, we have tended to use feminine pronouns. Although care givers certainly may be male, in this society mothers and other females continue to have the primary responsibility for children's care. When speaking of adoptees, we have used both genders interchangeably whenever we could not avoid a gender reference.
- Grammar—The English language lacks gender-neutral third-person singular pronouns. The impersonal singular pronouns

in our language are masculine. The authors deplore this constraint, but feel the use of "him/her" and similar artificial constructions would impede the flow of the text. Therefore, for readability and clarity, we have alternated between "him" and "her" and ask that readers understand.

The authors welcome queries and comments. Please address all correspondence to

Carole A. McKelvey and Dr. JoEllen Stevens
P.O. Box 1133
Oakview, CA 93022-1133

INTRODUCTION

Adoption.

For many the word represents hope and joy. Every year Americans adopt more than 100,000 children, 61,000 of whom are complete strangers. Another 440,000 people—grandparents, siblings and other family members—are touched by these adoption connections.

Connections are really what adoption is all about and, in many cases, these new bonds are fruitful and lifelong. In an alarming number of cases, however, the essential attachments and connections never develop. Adoptions have been failing at an accelerating rate in the past several decades, leaving critics of the current adoption system demanding change.

The national news has covered stories of parents returning unmanageable children to adoption agencies, of couples filing "wrongful adoption" lawsuits against agencies they say deceived them about the emotional histories of their adopted children and of black market baby-sellers taking advantage of infants in war torn foreign countries.

It is true that children available for adoption in the United States today are tougher than in past decades because they have more severe emotional problems that make them more difficult to parent. This is a direct consequence of the family distress in America and the welfare system set up to relieve it. Children who once were considered "unadoptable" and were consigned to a life in foster care have now been channeled into an adoption system unequipped to handle them.

In 1993, more than half the children waiting to be adopted were considered high risk because of problems they were born with or that have developed over years in abusive homes or in a long series of short-term foster homes. Many have languished in the system for years while waiting for permanent homes, developing mental problems that may keep them from succeeding if they finally do find parents.

CHILDREN WHO WAIT

The National Adoption Center prepared the following statistics based on children registered on their network as of March 22, 1991:

- 67% of the children are black or black/white.
- 52% of the children have some emotional problems.
- 32% of the children have some degree of learning disability.
- White children have more disabilities than black, with 71% having emotional problems.
- The largest age group is between five and eleven.
- The black children are younger, with 54% under eleven, compared to 31% for white children.
- There is a predominance of boys—almost two-thirds male.
- In total, 42% of the children are members of sibling groups.
- The average age of black children on the network is 10.2 years; white children average 12.6 years.

Because of birth control, abortion and unwed mothers who now keep more babies than they give up, the supply of healthy newborns available for adoption has all but dried up in the United States. Prospective parents who turn to foreign orphans have their own unique adoption problems, as do those who take American infants born with such defects as *in utero* drug exposure, fetal alcohol syndrome and HIV infection.

If you believe the worst-case scenarios, as many as half of all adoptions now end in failure. More study is needed to find out why, but it is clear that these factors contribute to a successful adoption:

- Youth (older children have a harder time adjusting to an adoptive home);
- A minimum number of moves and foster placements (frequent moves traumatize children);
- A permanency plan developed immediately after the child enters the system;
- Preplacement services to assess the family strengths and skills, and to ease the transition;
- A correct temperament match between parents and child;
- Full disclosure of the child's history and a realistic appraisal of the disruption risk;
- Postplacement intervention before problems become crises;
- Ongoing training and support for parents, lasting through adolescence in "special-needs" adoptions.

According to the North American Council on Adoptable Children, the authority on adoption in America and Canada, research underscores the fact that families who receive ongoing support and services are much more stable than those who do not.[1]

The reality is that such services are hard to get. In too many cases, overloaded caseworkers have dumped high-risk children on unsuspecting families, declaring that "all these children need is love and support." That simply isn't true.

In this book, the reader will find out what "special-needs" children are and how they can answer the prayers of infertile couples now turning to adoption for the children they desire. A word of warning: The foster care/adoption system they are trapped inside is fraught with problems that can bring heartache and broken dreams to people uninformed about the perils. With knowledge comes power and the ability to make a successful adoption choice.

We will discuss the landmark court decisions that established the rights of adoptive families to full disclosure of their children's congenital, environmental and hereditary problems. We also will highlight research being done about the role heredity plays in forming personality, how loving parents and a healthy home can come together to change a child's fate and how early intervention can alleviate the suffering of children exposed *in utero* to drugs, alcohol and HIV.

The reader will find out about matching techniques that fit the child to the family, and the unique situations caused by multicultural adoption, whether the child is foreign-born or American. The reader will also find stories of brave adoptive parents who share their triumphs, challenges, insights and truths.

Adoption Crisis unflinchingly raises issues about a welfare system that will allow nearly one million children to languish in foster care homes, detention centers and treatment facilities by the year 1995. Each additional day these lost children spend in the system exacts a toll on their ability to love and be loved. Many will never find an anchor in life's stormy sea. If we do nothing, their childhoods will continue to slip away in one temporary placement after another. We have ideas about how to help, and they all begin with reforming the business in which children are the commodity.

This book is dedicated to adoptive parents and their children. We hope it will increase the chances of children finding permanent, safe homes and of parents finding the children they can love. America's most valuable resource is its children; today we are tossing them aside at an unprecedented rate.

---

[1] The North American Council on Adoptable Children, *Adoptalk* (Spring 1993): p. 4.

ADOPTION CRISIS

THE SYSTEM

CHAPTER ONE

AN ADOPTION OVERVIEW

*It is the truth that truth
comes with its own consequences.*
Anonymous

Anyone pondering the adoption system in mid-1993 could think of only one thing—little Jessica DeBoer. The sensational case of the little girl caught between adoptive and birth parents who desperately struggled for custody captured the hearts of the nation in July, 1993.

One month later, the U.S. Supreme Court agreed with judges in two states, ruling that two-and-a-half-year-old Jessica be taken from the only parents she had ever known and returned to her birth parents. Experts across the country agreed that Jessica would suffer unimaginable harm from the move but, as lawyers told Supreme Court Justice Harry Blackmun,

> Jessica's case is about the inhumane consequences that
> will be inflicted on an innocent child whose welfare
> was never considered.[1]

Lawyers for Jessica asked the Supreme Court to recognize that children enjoy a constitutional right to have their "best interests" considered, in spite of family relationships. Instead, the court voted 6–2 to support the rights of Jessica's blood relatives, even though the ruling could harm her for life. Justice Blackmun, who with Sandra Day O'Connor cast a dissenting vote, wrote that the case "touches the raw nerves of life's relationships."[2] Indeed.

In fact, it appears that no one really considered the consequences to little Jessica, neither her birth parents, her adoptive parents nor the courts. But that's not unusual. Every day children are removed as abruptly from their homes and placed with people they have never met. This case is a classic example of how children in America are treated—as possessions.

Jessica's sad saga began February 8, 1991, when an unmarried woman from Blairstown, Iowa, gave birth to her. Naming the wrong man as the child's father, Cara Schmidt signed relinquishment papers shortly after birth, and Roberta and Jan DeBoer of Ann Arbor, Michigan, took the child home. Later Cara revealed to Daniel Schmidt that he was the true father and, less than a month later, they began trying to get their daughter back.

Daniel Schmidt, who later married Cara, charged that he never signed away his parental rights. Two state courts and the U.S. Supreme Court agreed with him, and in early August, 1993, Jessica DeBoer became Anna Schmidt and returned to Iowa with her birth parents.

While examining the subject on television's "Nightline," guest host Barbara Walters asked the obvious question of her guests: "Just how long a time period should there be after which birth parents can not change their minds?"[3] Guests who both supported and opposed the Supreme Court ruling said the waiting time should be no longer than six months, during which time the birth mother should be responsible for contacting the birth father.

This waiting period would not have prevented Jessica's problem, however, because Cara Schmidt filed a motion to get her daughter back only twenty-six days after the child was born. The case was then dragged out in court until the child was two and a half. Both the birth parents and the adoptive parents had the opportunity to save Jessica this heartache at any point along the way, but they chose not to.

This case touched the hearts of millions, who watched helplessly as the little girl and her families suffered. Those who could think of no other way to cry out wrote thousands of letters to magazines and newspapers around the country. On August 9, 1993, *Time* magazine printed excerpts from the letters it received, most expressing despair at the outcome and the pain it caused. One, from California Supreme Court Judge Eric E. Younger, tried to offer comfort. He wrote that "statutes favoring the birth parents most often produce results with which we're all comfortable (or at least less uncomfortable)." He noted that judges are not magicians, although we wish they were. The little girl's struggles also became fodder for a made for TV movie that highlighted the highly publicized Baby Jessica custody case.

Looking at the case with hindsight, the authors believe an agreement known as "mediated adoption" might have saved everyone involved from their turmoil. This new procedure allows all parties to play a role in their child's upbringing, letting them mediate details such as visitation and parental contact before the child is relinquished. At the least, this might have allowed Jessica the chance to develop a relationship with her birth parents before having to move in with them.

As it was, the image of Jessica, sobbing as she was driven away from her Ann Arbor home, was imprinted in the minds of a nation. She wasn't the only one crying. Through her tears, Roberta DeBoer told reporters that "a child addresses people who care for her on a constant basis as Mom and Dad. I hope Dan and Cara realize there is no replacement for Mom and Dad."[4]

Thousands of couples hoping to adopt also felt a catch in their throats. With such dramatic evidence that birth parents can regain their children, many grew reluctant to open themselves up to such sorrow.

And although their cases don't make the news, children are removed from their parents just as abruptly and with just as much trauma every day, in every state. While these actions may ostensibly be taken in an effort to protect the child, the trauma to the child caused by abrupt removal may be lifelong.

At the same time, the two million couples who eventually turn to adoption find a system short on healthy infants and heavy on older children who have a variety of problems. The reasons:

■ *Single women are relinquishing fewer babies for adoption.*
More young adults are using birth control, and some of those who don't are aborting unplanned children. Because single

parenthood has become acceptable in our society, even more are choosing to raise their own babies.

- *Sexually transmitted diseases have increased.* Transgressions of the "Free Love '60s and '70s" are coming back to haunt couples in the form of infertility caused by sexually transmitted diseases.
- *Couples have put off having a family for a variety of reasons, including career development.* As women age, their fertility decreases, and as the country's 75-plus million baby boomers reach middle age, their infertility rate is soaring. National newspapers recently declared an infertility epidemic, with nearly 5 million American women infertile. The biological time clocks of another 21 million American women will stop ticking during the first decade of the twenty-first century, according to a congressional hearing, as they reach menopause.[5] Those who still want children will be motivated to adopt.
- *The adoption system is overrun with children who have special needs but has little money to recruit, train and support families willing to adopt them.* Only one of every one hundred couples interested in adopting can hope to find a healthy, Caucasian infant in this country.

Most of the available children are classified as "Special-Needs Adoptees" because they are older, are members of minority groups, are members of a sibling group that must stay together or are in some way physically or mentally challenged. Two new groups of children joined this category in the '90s:

- *Drug-exposed infants.* Anglo and minority infants exposed to a plethora of drugs in the womb—including alcohol and crack cocaine—represent a growing number of available children.
- *Infants born HIV positive.* Many are destined to get AIDS.

Because of these changes, the emphasis in the adoption world has changed. Whereas emphasis once was on providing healthy babies to childless couples, the focus now is on finding suitable parents for children who are "genetically fragile," older and with special needs.

SPECIAL NEEDS IN AMERICA:
WHO ARE AMERICA'S ORPHANS?

- Those over the age of five in the foster care system.
- Children of various races, including mixed-race children.
- Sibling groups who must be adopted together.
- Handicapped or otherwise challenged children, either physically, mentally or emotionally.

Today there are 500,000 such children in America who are waiting for homes—children who are emotionally deprived and who can be compared to the little ones still locked inside cold orphanages in Romania. They can't wait any longer. Someone must help them.

Although the nation's adoption system was designed to do just that, it has lost its effectiveness. But no discussion of adoption is complete without first examining the foster care system into which most adoptable children first go. It is overwhelmed with a growing number of special-needs children, many of whom are trapped in the system by parents who will not relinquish them for adoption. Those who have not been abused and neglected before they enter the system are damaged by repeated moves, developing attachment disorders that prevent them from getting close to anyone.

Although the welfare system is understaffed and overwhelmed, it receives the lion's share of the federal money earmarked for child welfare. The adoption system, on the other hand, designed to find homes for those children rescued from bad situations, has few resources for supporting the families who agree to adopt these children. It can't provide enough help to prevent adoptions from going sour, nor does it work to ensure good matches between parents and children by using temperament and genetic tests.

The Federal Adoption Assistance Act, passed in 1980, is partly to blame. It required social service agencies to increase their efforts to find homes for children previously thought to be unadoptable. Until that time, these children with special needs were raised in foster homes until they were old enough to emancipate. This law offered financial incentives for families willing to adopt needy children, and courts became slightly more willing to make neglected or abused children available for adoption by forcing parents to relinquish their rights.

The Federal Adoption Assistance Act released a whole new group of children into a system inadequately prepared to handle them. Social services and adoption agencies had little experience in working with special-needs adoptions and the new wave of adoptees it produced. In Minnesota, for example, a state with one of the highest adoption rates in the nation, only 4 percent of the children adopted in 1970 by nonrelatives were identified as special-needs children. In 1986, however, more than 50 percent were in that category. Minnesota's experience is being duplicated in states across the nation.[6]

At the same time, the numbers of children in out-of-home placements in the United States (either foster homes, therapeutic settings or juvenile justice facilities) soared. By 1995, more than 550,000 children were expected to be in the foster care system alone, with another 290,000 in mental health or juvenile justice facilities.[7] Unfortunately, these children are being funneled into a decreasing number of foster care homes, and programs designed to help them return to their birth homes are scarce and underfunded.

Adoption workers know it is difficult to find parents who can stretch their expectations, especially to accommodate these very difficult children. Although they do so in a misguided effort to find homes for the children, too many ignore the importance of finding a good "family match" for these lost children, and too many "forget" to tell adoptive parents the complete truth about their children's disabilities. Both can bring disastrous results.

The increase in adoptions that fail is a nasty secret in America. As special-needs children are bounced from one foster care home to another, their ability to adjust to an adoptive family declines. Often they bring more challenges than an average family can cope with. Families that originally welcomed their children with open arms learn over time just how troubling these challenges can be. Art and Jenny Scovis of California found out the hard way.

LELAND'S STORY

Like many American couples, Jenny and Art Scovis looked for a child beyond U.S. borders to add to their family. They found two-year-old Leland in Korea with the help of the worldwide adoption agency, Adoption International. "We got a picture of him ... that looked like he had a mouthful of cookies," says Jenny Scovis. "His mouth was pushed out. Anyway, that is all I knew about him."[8]

They arranged to have him sent halfway around the world, from an orphanage in a small Korean town to a suburb of Los Angeles. When Leland toddled off the airplane, the family's long journey was just beginning. When they embraced the dark-haired child with almond-shaped eyes, they had no idea they would be unable to save him.

Unlike their fantasies of a perfect child, Leland was a trauma-tized toddler who had been abandoned at age one and had been in six foster homes before he arrived at the orphanage a year later. There he got little attention and little nourishment, although his adoptive parents wouldn't find that out for many years.

When Leland first saw his adoptive father, "he screamed bloody murder," Art says. "I don't think he had seen someone with a beard before." And even though the child threw temper tantrums that lasted three or four hours at a time, Jenny called him "my gift from God" and "the child of my heart."

"And he was," she says. "It didn't matter what color or what religion, we just wanted a boy under three years old. That was our main requirement ... [although we also asked] that he not have a men-tal deficiency. Neither Art nor I thought we could deal with that." Jenny laughs. "As it turns out, he had severe learning disabilities. We ended up dealing with it anyway."

In the beginning, however, the family focused on the immediate problems. Leland was malnourished and had a distended stomach. He was scared by everything and wouldn't sleep. For the first several months Jenny slept on the floor with him, listening to him cry, "Uma, Uma," Korean for mother, Jenny supposed.

Then one night the couple couldn't quiet him. Art said to Jenny, "Take off your clothes and let him feel some skin." She did, and although she didn't have any milk, Leland started to nurse. He regressed in behavior to that of an infant, crawling instead of walking and babbling like a baby. Eventually he calmed down.

"Those first few months were a nightmare," Jenny remembers. "I was studying for the bar [exam], and I'm not surprised I failed it."

After the immediate problems subsided, however, emotional and learning problems surfaced. Jenny believes Leland was damaged by a lack of protein during his early years. In any case, Leland had trouble putting things in sequence and scored so low in some subjects he was "off the charts at the bottom," she says.

"We gave him hell for awhile because we didn't realize he had learning disabilities," says Art. "We didn't know any better. We wouldn't have done it if we had known." Once they did find out, the couple arranged for him to have educational therapy twice a week.

Leland's emotional problems also seemed to be endless. One day the couple got a call from the school office saying Leland had mutilated his arm. "The cuts were very, very deep," says Jenny. Leland explained them to her by saying, "I don't know, it's like I go into a fog, and I can't control it."

Jenny was frightened by the child's dark side, a place she could never reach. One part of him didn't "go for people," and another lacked empathy for animals. "We bought Lee some animals," Jenny says, "and he just was not caring about them." That dark side probably came from the many moves and bonding breaks he had had as a baby.

After a rough spell when Leland was twelve and thirteen, the boy seemed to blossom as he neared his fourteenth birthday. His grades were improving, "he was becoming defined, and I was accepting the definition," Art says. "He was really coming into his own. It was nice to see."

Art and Jenny Scovis saw this progress as a sign that they had successfully come through the worst times with their special-needs child. Then the phone call came.

"Mr. and Mrs. Scovis?" the voice on the line said. "Your son has been taken by helicopter to Westlake Medical Center in Westlake Village. He is in very serious condition, and you need to come as soon as possible."

Leland had not been in a car accident. On a dare, he had chugged 2–3 inches of alcohol from a gallon jug. Witnesses said two brothers, who were chaperoning a group of teenagers at Leo Carrillo State Beach, bet Leland that he couldn't drink the remaining alcohol without getting sick. He drank the alcohol rapidly, collapsing fifteen minutes later. By the time his parents reached the hospital, he was in a coma. On April 16, 1990, Leland Scovis died of alcohol poisoning at the age of fourteen. The chaperones were convicted of his death and sentenced to community service.

Jenny talks through tears about her regrets—that Leland was left on the beach without help for two hours after collapsing, that she would never see him grow to adulthood. "We were so proud we overcame his poor beginning," she says, which makes it even more difficult to come to terms with the tragic way his life ended.

Reflecting on his son's death, Art says: "This parental relationship, which was basically our last full-time parenting relationship, just never managed to take off. It's just all of a sudden been ripped from us. I am not [a parent]. That is very hard for me to deal with."

Leland's parents believed he was just beginning to come into his own, but they will never know. Perhaps from Leland's perspective the future seemed less bright. They don't know why Leland Scovis drank the alcohol that night on the beach, or why a few months earlier he had mutilated his arm. No one knows what Leland, like so many other adopted children, went through before coming to his new family. No one knows what really went on inside the head of this child. We only know that it left him a troubled youth who died a sad death at fourteen.

OVERSEAS IMPACT

The Scovises were not infertile and had older children before adopting Leland to refeather their nest. Most parents who look outside the U.S. borders are infertile, however, and are looking for healthy infants. In the mid-1990s, Americans began to look across the oceans in countries decimated by war or disaster.

In the 1980s, they focused on children in Korea, adopting more than twenty thousand before the Korean government put on the brakes in 1988. Then their attention turned to children languishing in

Romanian orphanages. After several years of chaos, Romanian officials also stopped the flow of children until they could develop a system for the orderly adoption of infants, which they did in 1993. In the mid-1990s, attention swung to Bosnia, formerly Yugoslavia, and to the hapless youngsters caught in the war and famine on the African continent. Few of these children were available for adoption, however.

Parents who have adopted foreign children say it has been a worthwhile experience, but one that brings its own set of unique problems. The authors meet the news of foreign adoption with mixed feelings. With caseworkers struggling to place the half million American special-needs children waiting for families, it is hard to justify looking to other lands for children. We can not escape our problems by turning to children in other countries, nor can we deny the adoption crisis in our own country. When we do, we ignore the needs of children here at home.

NEW ADOPTION AGENDAS

In *Adoption Crisis*, the authors will examine the system that can unknowingly abuse the children it is set up to protect. Children who have been moved a number of times prior to adoption, who were abused or neglected in the first two years of life or who are older than five years probably have learned not to love. They arrive in adoptive homes unable to respond to stability or love, and bent on maintaining chaos and perpetuating hostility in the family.[9] An unusually large number of adopted children fall within this category.

The truth is that many of them are "unadoptable" as we know the term today, although well-meaning caseworkers sometimes are reluctant to accept that fact. They often tell potential parents that love and a stable home are all the child needs, although this is a simplistic approach to complex problems.

Too many mental health professionals discount the effect attachment disorders can have on a family. Even though they do so with the good intention of finding children homes, downplaying or withholding background information about children are mistakes that can lead to dumping dangerous children into the laps of unsuspecting adoptive parents.

Unless their parents are trained to deal with their problems and get an enormous amount of postadoption support, some of these children would be best served in therapeutic settings. Unable to love as toddlers, these children can embrace hatred as teenagers and adults. What we as a nation don't realize is that these children are time bombs ready to go off. They are capable of growing up to become the nation's psychopaths, and when they explode, it will be the nation that pays the price.

One promising new approach to the adoption of infants is being pioneered by Dr. Jeanne Etter of Eugene, Oregon. Called "mediated adoption," it provides a way for children to preserve all their family bonds—with adoptive as well as birth parents. Etter and Martin Giovanni tracked 129 birth and adoptive parents involved in fifty-six open adoptions and were heartened by the results. They selected children adopted between 1984 and 1987, most adopted as infants through mediated open adoptions and representing most cultural and racial backgrounds. All adoptive parents were Caucasian. They found that:

- Participants reported high levels of cooperation, with 98.2 percent of birth and adoptive parents keeping their mediated agreements with respect to visits;
- More than 75 percent reported no conflict in their relationships.[10]

The mediated adoptions allowed all parties a say in how and when contact would be made. Etter and Giovanni found that an astounding 92.9 percent of the participants kept their agreements, and only 25 percent experienced conflict. That is particularly surprising because custody disputes in general are increasing as birth parents insist on having input into their children's fate. Escalating conflict can lead to "outcome damaging to children, families and society," Etter and Giovanni write.[11]

To be successful, they say, mediated adoptions must include:

- Counseling for birth parents on their options;
- Education for adoptive parents;
- The opportunity for birth parents and adoptive parents to choose each other;

- The chance to plan the amount and type of contact birth parents will have, with results included in a written mediation agreement; and
- The opportunity for all parties to make a final decision after the child is born.

Obviously, this process only works for couples adopting infants. For those people involved with the rest of the children, many questions remain unanswered.

- Who will step forward to adopt the children with special needs and how will they prepare themselves for the challenge?
- How can the adoption industry make it easier for infertile couples or other potential parents to adopt special-needs children?
- Should the system continue to reject prospective parents, including many minority families, simply because they can't afford the $2,000–$5,000 it takes to pay adoption fees?
- Why does the system deny homes to children of color simply because they can not find minority families? Should white couples be allowed to give homes to these minority and mixed-race youngsters so they can have a stable home environment?
- What influences do genetics have on adoptees? Are we more influenced by nature or nurture? What do adoptive parents need to know about this emerging field?
- How do we make it possible for a family to achieve a satisfactory "family fit" or match? How do we convince the industry that this step is necessary for success?
- What can be done about attachment problems with adopted children? Can these attachment problems (the inability to love and bond with a parent or significant other) be prevented or remedied?
- How should society deal with drug-exposed and HIV-infected infants?
- How are adolescent and adult adoptees helped to cope with loss and grieving issues?
- Where can adoptive families turn for help in getting through the adoption maze?

The reality of adoption as we approach the turn of the century is that America's children—its future—are suffering, and it is those children who need our love and attention now. Parents seeking children must "stretch their expectations" to include a child who may be a far different one from the "fantasy child" they originally sought. Likewise, the system must stretch its imagination to find new answers for damaged and perhaps "unadoptable" children. With even more innovation, perhaps we can prevent the damage in the first place. It's a challenge we all must face.

---

[1] Associated Press, "Custody Battle over Michigan Girl Back in Court," *Denver Rocky Mountain News*, July 29, 1993, p. 38.

[2] Mary Deibel, Scripps Howard News Service, *Denver Rocky Mountain News*, July 31, 1993, p. 42.

[3] Barbara Walters, "Nightline," August 1993.

[4] Associated Press, *The Denver Post*, July 4, 1993.

[5] *Update* (April 1991).

[6] Michael Orlans, "Adoption: An American Crisis," *Attachments* (Spring 1993).

[7] U.S. House Select Committee on Children, Youth and Families, "No Place to Call Home: Discarded Children in America," December 11, 1989.

[8] Jenny and Art Scovis, personal interview, Oxnard, California, January 1990.

[9] U.S. House Select Committee on Children, Youth and Families, "No Place to Call Home."

[10] Jeanne Etter and Martin Giovanni, *Documentation Project: The Success Rate of Mediated Adoption Agreements, 1990 Pilot Study of 56 Open Adoptions*, p. 2.

[11] Ibid., p. 6.

CHAPTER TWO

THE BABY CHASE

Never shalt thou the heavens see,
Save as a little child thou be.
Lanier, *The Symphony*

About 240 babies a year are released for adoption at the nation's largest maternity home and adoption agency, the Edna Gladney Center in Fort Worth, Texas, and every year more than four thousand couples inquire about adopting them. That works out to nearly seventeen potential families for every available child.

Though dramatic, those figures are not unusual. The demand for children in the United States is so steep that at least twenty prospective couples apply for each adoptable child.[1] Each year more than one million couples wait for children, yet only twenty-five thousand infants are available to them.

Adoptable newborns in the United States are in short supply, for a number of reasons. Nearly 30 percent of all pregnancies were terminated in 1989, and of the 3.8 million children carried to term that year, nearly one-fourth (878,477) were born to unmarried women. Less than 3 percent of those children were released for adoption.[2]

At the same time, 4.5 million American couples have infertility problems, and thousands of others (figures haven't been compiled) also want to adopt children, including single people and fertile couples with a humanitarian desire to aid homeless children. Their desire to adopt and the shortage of newborns have resulted in a full-scale baby chase that has sent some prospective parents to the classified sections of college newspapers, and others on around-the-world recruiting missions. It has driven some to spend thousands of dollars on medical miracles and others to spend almost as much on "gray market" baby businesses.

INFERTILE COUPLES ON THE CHASE

For 75-plus million baby boomers, biological time is running out. Since the mid-1960s, the number of married women under the age of thirty who have never had a baby has doubled, and after the age of thirty the chance of conception declines rapidly. One in six couples find themselves infertile because of advancing age, environmental pollution, sexually transmitted diseases or pelvic inflammatory disease caused by IUDs. (After three episodes of pelvic inflammatory disease, the rate of infertility more than doubles.)[3] In 1987, Americans spent about $1 billion on medical care to combat infertility. Recent scientific breakthroughs, such as *in vitro* fertilization (IVF) and gamete intra-Fallopian transfer (GIFT) have given them reason to hope for a miracle.

Those techniques have made it possible for a few previously infertile couples to conceive and carry a child to term, but researchers warn that they are expensive and usually don't result in pregnancy. Only 200,000 babies are born each year to couples using advanced infertility treatments.[4]

Research done by Janice G. Raymond, a professor of women's studies and medical ethics at the University of Massachusetts, found that between 90 and 95 percent of all women undergoing IVF are unsuccessful. "In the United States there is still no accurate assessment of live-baby rates," Raymond told a *Ms.* magazine reporter. "The 1989 Wyden Congressional Subcommittee reported a 9 percent 'take-home baby' success rate for IVF. Many clinics report success, but do not mention live births."[5]

Also unknown are the number of *healthy* children born using IVF, although some research suggests the process results in increased rates of premature births and low-birth-weight babies. An Australian study found the mortality rate for children conceived through IVF was 47.5 deaths in the first twenty-eight days after birth for every one thousand births. That rate is four times higher than that for non-IVF births.

Despite those dismal success rates, IVF treatments are now offered at more than two hundred U.S. institutions, Janice Raymond said. "A large number of these centers are for-profit 'fertility institutes' that perform other reproductive services, such as surrogacy and sex predetermination as well."[6] Their prices usually start at $5,000 per cycle, and many women return as many as ten times before they give up. Few, if any, medical insurance plans pay for the procedure.

If that technique doesn't work, some couples are eligible for gamete intra-Fallopian transfer, a process that involves injecting eggs and sperm into a woman's Fallopian tubes. Like IVF, it can fail to result in a fetus or it can result in too many.

THE BAASCH BABIES

In 1989, Sharyl Baasch of Denver, Colorado, was injected with nine eggs and 100,000 of her husband Steve's sperm. Dr. Richard Worley told the couple there was no way to know how many of the nine eggs would become fertilized. In Sharyl's case, five grew into healthy fetuses.

Although twenty-nine-year-old Sharyl was healthy, carrying all five babies to term would be tricky. The couple considered "fetal reduction," the controversial process that destroys one or more of the developing fetuses by injecting them with sodium chloride or an air bubble, but then rejected it.

"I wanted to find out how to get through my pregnancy, not how to eliminate babies," Baasch told the *Rocky Mountain News*.[7] On August 31, 1990, the couple's healthy quintuplets were born at Denver's AMI St. Luke's Hospital.

Multiple births are never the goal, Dr. Worley said after the Baasch delivery. "The best result is one baby, and there's no good reason to pursue more than twins."[8] The odds against carrying five babies beyond the crucial twenty-eight-week gestation period are astronomical, and babies who do survive the early stages can arrive prematurely with severe neurological problems or underdeveloped lungs.

When last-ditch efforts fail to produce a pregnancy, couples who still want a family must turn to others for their children. In a process that combines medical technology and the help of strangers, surrogacy is the answer for some.

THE SURROGACY CONTROVERSY

It seems like such a simple concept—hiring a fertile woman to carry the child of an infertile couple. So far an estimated six hundred to one thousand children have been born in the United States to surrogate mothers who are artificially inseminated or surgically implanted with another couple's embryo.[9]

The jury is still out on the ethics of the country's newest "cottage" industry, in which mothers often get $10,000 for their unique "baby-sitting" services. Should the surrogate mother have custody or visitation rights to the child, or is she merely a unique kind of "foster home" in which someone else's baby is kept? Is she providing a humanitarian service or leasing her womb?

The "Baby M" case in New Jersey may be the most widely publicized surrogacy dispute, in which surrogate mother Mary Beth Whitehead-Gould sued for custody of the child she bore for William and Elizabeth Stern. She was paid $10,000 for carrying the child, plus $20,000 in additional expenses, but later decided she wanted to keep the child.

The New Jersey Supreme Court awarded the child to Stern, but ruled that Whitehead-Gould was the genetic mother because she provided the egg that was artificially inseminated with Stern's sperm. She was given visitation rights, but they were later terminated after she fled to Florida with the child.[10]

The court also ruled that such surrogacy contracts are void and against public policy, with Chief Justice Robert N. Wilentz calling them "baby-selling" and not in the best interest of the child.

Reactions to the ruling were widespread, with some calling surrogacy the "commercial" lease of a woman's womb and others supporting the fee as just compensation for the mother's time and energy spent during the pregnancy. One surrogate mother who supports the court ruling is thirty-five-year-old Patti Foster who, in 1985, saw an ad in the *Detroit News* that offered $10,000 to "carry a couple's child."

Foster says she thought it would be a charitable thing to do, plus the money was attractive, but several things made her hesitate. She and her husband fought all the way to the attorney's office, where they went to discuss the details. At first, Foster thought she would be implanted with the couple's embryo, but then she found out she would have to supply the egg and be the child's genetic mother. She started to back out, she told a reporter from *For Women First* magazine, but the lawyer "convinced me it was the right thing to do."

Then Foster didn't hit it off with the couple. The more the baby grew, the more she felt her body wasn't her own. "My child wasn't my own, either," she said. "My body, my baby, my life were all under someone else's control." When she explained her fears to attorney Noel Keane, he told her, "Jesus was a surrogate birth."[11]

The day she had to give up the child was the worst day of her life, she said. "I cried and cried. But I didn't have a choice." Although she filed for custody, it was denied and her appeals were denied. "The only time I see my son is by accident, on the street," she said. "Someday he's going to find out the truth ... that he was bred and bought."[12]

Since then, more than twenty states have scrambled to pass laws that control surrogacy, and judges throughout the country have had to struggle with custody issues when surrogates and genetic parents disagree. Kentucky, Indiana, Louisiana, Florida, Michigan, Nebraska and Utah now ban surrogate pregnancies, and a California judge ruled in 1990 that "genetics is the primary criterion of parenthood."[13] In that case, Mark and Crispina Calvert supplied the egg and the sperm that were implanted in Anna Johnson's uterus after she signed a $10,000 contract.

Judge Richard Parslow of Orange County Superior Court ruled on October 22, 1990, that Johnson had served in the role of a foster parent, and the child was ordered to remain in the custody of his genetic parents. The judge also denied visitation to Johnson, saying, "A three-parent, two-natural mom situation is ripe for crazy-making ... I decline to split the child emotionally between two mothers."[14]

In what may be an even more bizarre case of surrogacy, a forty-two-year-old South Dakota woman carried the children of her daughter, who could not bear children. In 1991, Arlette Schweitzer of Aberdeen, South Dakota, gave birth to her own healthy twin grandchildren after being implanted with eggs removed from her daughter and fertilized with her son-in-law's sperm. A South African woman beat her to the punch, however, giving birth to her daughter's triplets in 1987.

Not all surrogate pregnancies go sour and end up in court, however. Thirty-year-old Kathy Stovall formed a lasting friendship with the couple whose twins she carried in 1986. She had wanted to volunteer her uterus since she first heard of the concept in the early '80s, and thought the money would be nice, too. She discovered that $10,000 "for a 24-hour-a-day job for nearly a year isn't much," she wrote in *For Women First* magazine. "It just gets you by."[15]

Stovall applied at the New England Center for Surrogate Parenting in 1986, an agency that required surrogates to have children of their own, to have never given up a child for adoption and to have the agreement of their husbands. She explained the pregnancy to her two-year-old child as "baby-sitting, but in a different way."

When Linda and Glenn Merkel were put in touch with Stovall, they already had a son Brad who was born for them by another surrogate mother. Linda was unable to carry a child because of a cancer operation but was able to provide an egg that was fertilized *in vitro* by her husband's sperm. It cost the couple $50,000 to fertilize the egg and implant it in Stovall's uterus, but most of the cost was covered by health insurance.

To everyone's surprise, Kathy Stovall wound up carrying the couple's twins. "I admit I was stunned at first," she said. "Twins can be rough on your body, but Linda was always there to help. She and Glenn came out five times in nine months to see how I was." The twins, Kimberly and Brent, were born healthy and into the arms of their mother, Linda—at Stovall's insistence.

"Being a surrogate mother meant I'd been touched by a miracle," Stovall said. "I love the whole Merkel family, but it's not like we're related. We're best friends."[16] And when Kathy Stovall had a little girl of her own in January, 1991, Linda Merkel was there to help her.

Because of the cost, legal hassles and moral issues, surrogacy is not a choice for most couples seeking children. Many turn to private adoption, aggressively seeking a pregnant teen willing to assign them

her baby rather than passively waiting for newborns to cycle through
the public agencies.

ADVERTISING FOR BABIES

> *Loving & secure professional Calif. couple wishes*
> *to adopt newborn. Will pay all costs.*
> *Collect 714-522-2694/attorney 714-841-3444.*

Charlene and Steve Sugarman, a California couple, placed this
ad in the University of Colorado's Boulder campus newspaper. Like
other aggressive couples trying to adopt a baby, they were using a
direct approach. Ads such as theirs are common in college and alternative newspapers throughout the country, and *The Daily Pennsylva-
nian* has a permanent classified ad category titled "Adoptions."

It's not a new idea. Wilma and Bob Hahn of Berthoud, Colorado, were one of the first couples to find a baby through a newspaper
ad. Their 1957 ad in *The Denver Post* caught the eye of a single mother
in Texas, who allowed them to adopt her child, Cindy.

Any parent who actively seeks a child must walk a fine line between "baby-hunting" and "baby-buying." In many states, it is only
legal for prospective parents to pay legal and medical expenses directly related to adoption, usually averaging $9,000–$10,000. Not all
states allow independent adoptions, and only a few allow attorneys to
handle independent or private adoptions.

State laws are an attempt to avoid blatant baby-selling rings like
those uncovered in Texas and Arizona in the 1980s. They were the
worst-case scenarios of what can happen when innovative entrepre-
neurs meet up with desperate prospective parents.

BUYING BABIES

In 1985, an Arizona woman was convicted of operating a Mexican adoption pipeline, and for alleged mail and wire fraud. She had
bilked 180 couples in forty states out of an estimated $750,000, and
provided only a few of them with children.

In 1988, a Dallas lawyer was convicted of buying a child for a client who privately adopted the child. The same year, another Texas man was convicted of buying three children and selling them to adoptive parents.

In 1991, American couples were accused of bribing middlemen and taxi drivers to find them adoptable babies in Romania.[17]

"There are people out there who would give almost anything to have a child," United States Senator Bob Dole (R-Kansas) explained, and there are almost as many people willing to help them find one. Many do business in Texas because the lax laws on private adoption make possible a "gray market" in which violations can occur but are difficult to prove.

The state also leads the nation in the number of children available for adoption each year, according to Jeff Rosenberg of the National Committee for Adoption.[18] "We know that women get cars to give up their babies, or shopping sprees or college scholarships," he said. "Some of them make a very good living."

One birth mother, for example, testified in 1988 that a Dallas lawyer paid her more than $2,000 for rent, groceries, maternity clothes and taxi fares during her pregnancy in 1984. In exchange, she gave him the baby. Texas laws allow attorneys to handle the legal paperwork in an adoption but prohibit them from putting adopting parents together with expectant mothers. The lawyer was convicted of baby-buying.

In another Texas case, sixty-one-year-old Robert I. Kingsley was sentenced to seven years in prison and fined $5,000 for selling a child to a New York couple for $14,000. The case is being appealed, but Kingsley is on probation for two more counts of baby-buying. On those charges he was sentenced to ten years probation, fined $1,000 and ordered to pay one couple $37,000 in restitution.

"It's fairly easy for someone to act as a go-between," said Bob Barker, director of Houston's DePelchin Children's Center. "It's a misdemeanor to act as a go-between, but it's a crime that is seldom reported."

Texas isn't the only place this kind of gray market operates. One of the largest was run from 1978 to 1983 by thirty-five-year-old Debbie Tanner of Wilcox, Arizona. She teamed up with two friends to charge

money for babies that, in most cases, were not delivered. Most of their
victims were Anglo couples living in Utah or Massachusetts who paid
between $300 and $6,000 for adoptable Mexican babies.

Chan Chaffin of Cortez, Colorado, said she and her husband
paid Tanner $3,500 for a three-year-old Mexican girl. The couple re-
modeled a bedroom and bought furniture and clothes for the child
who never arrived.

"[Tanner] kept promising and promising us a baby," Chaffin told
The Denver Post in 1985. "Finally, about a year ago, she wrote us a
letter and said she was going out of business. We never got our money
back and never got no [sic] baby, but the FBI came to see us."[19]

Tom and Kathy Lambson of New Mexico also turned to Tanner
for a child. Then in their late 30s, the couple had been unsuccessfully
trying to adopt for eight years when they heard of a woman who helped
people get unwanted babies from Mexico.

"People get desperate," Lambson said. "Adoption ... you know,
wanting children ... is a very emotional thing. Sometimes you just
don't see things for what they are."[20] They paid Tanner $4,000 for a
child who never came, then chalked it up to experience. Only when
the FBI began to investigate did they realize they weren't the only ones
who had been duped.

Another Manassa, Colorado, couple that did business with Tanner
actually received two children, but their birth mother, Ermilla Hernandez
of Mexico, now claims she was tricked into surrendering the girls.
Madalyn Sutherland and her husband legally adopted two Mexican
children in 1981, nine-year-old Paula and twelve-year-old Maria.

Perhaps the most bizarre story is of a man accused of being so
obsessed with having a child that he resorted to murder. In August,
1991, Ralph Takemire of Topeka, Kansas, was accused of killing a
family friend, nineteen-year-old Terra Ann Ikerd of Colorado, to kid-
nap her infant daughter. "Uncle Ralph," as Takemire was known, allegedly took the young mother and baby on a shopping trip, then shot
the mother and stole her twelve-week-old baby, Heather. The young
mother's body was found July 22 in a remote field, and authorities
originally thought the child also was dead.

A chance visit to Colorado by a Topeka detective lead to the
arrest of Takemire, who allegedly told police he was unable to impreg-

nate his girlfriend and so kidnapped the baby. Heather was found and on August 11 was delivered into the arms of her widowed father at Denver's Stapleton Airport by Topeka deputies.

Of course, Takemire's case is an extreme example of the lengths to which people will go for a baby. A more likely scenario involves finding a pregnant teenager and paying her expenses in exchange for the chance to adopt her baby.

A PRIVATE ADOPTION

The hospital hallways are dark on this gloomy fall Tuesday night in 1989. There have been seven births already tonight, and the staff is overwhelmed. In Room 228B, "Sandy" lies sad and exhausted. Several nights of false labor have taken their toll on this single eighteen-year-old woman, but tonight she is 3 centimeters dilated. This labor definitely isn't false, but the woman desperately needs sleep. Her doctor orders an epidural pain killer and something to help her sleep.

Sandy dozes off, but there is no sleep for the other woman in her room. "Linda Smith" is Sandy's birth coach—and the adoptive mother of this unborn baby. She has come here tonight to lend moral support. Her husband, "George," is out of town.

By 7 A.M. the birth process has come to a grinding halt, with no further dilation, no more contractions. Monitors show that the unborn baby is in distress. Also in distress is Linda, who has waited much longer for this moment than the teenage mother. She and her husband, who married at age thirty-nine, tried unsuccessfully to have children for four years before accepting the fact that her biological clock had stopped ticking.

Then they put the word out that they were seeking a child to adopt. They announced it everywhere they went, including the beauty parlor. Weeks later, Sandy's older sister called to say the girl was pregnant and might consider giving up the child. The child's father left the state when he found out Sandy was pregnant, and abortion was out of the question for religious reasons.

"Before I called Sandy, I called an attorney who handled these cases privately," Linda said.[21] "Then I asked Sandy to call [him ... He] knew what to ask her and how to proceed."

Under their state's laws, the Smiths were only allowed to pay for medical and legal costs related to the pregnancy. It was a hard law to follow, Linda admitted, "but you have to avoid any possibility someone might accuse you of buying the baby." Instead, she helped Sandy, who "didn't have anything, no money, nothing," by making her maternity jumpers and borrowing other maternity clothing from friends.

At first Linda wasn't worried that Sandy would back out. The teen's father had left her mother to raise eleven children alone, and "she had been in therapy about this," Linda said. "She felt strongly that a child needed two parents."

Not long afterwards, however, Sandy began to have doubts. "One time, after she started going to a relinquishment counselor, Sandy decided she really wanted to keep the baby," Linda said. "She told the counselor she felt everyone else was running her life and she was confused." Sandy did an immediate about-face, however, and proceeded with the relinquishment.

In her fourth month, Sandy began bleeding and panicked. The doctor thought she might be having a miscarriage so, to calm her down and keep an eye on her, Linda invited her to spend the night. That night Linda gained respect for the young woman who was willing to sacrifice her own happiness so that her child could have what she couldn't give it.

The miscarriage crisis passed. The couple settled into month after month of waiting and worrying about whether the child would be born safely. The Lamaze classes were particularly hard, with Linda attending as Sandy's coach. "All the other people were couples," she said. "Although there now are classes for single mothers, none was available when we needed it." One night Sandy "just sort of lost it," Linda said, and the Lamaze teacher thought she could be suicidal. The girl calmed down as they talked during the long drive home, Linda said.

The Smiths discussed it and decided to do what was best for Sandy, even if it meant letting her keep the baby. "After all, we were childless before this happened and we would be childless after," Linda said. George talked to Sandy about their decision, and the girl reassured him she wasn't going to back out.

Now, at the hospital, Sandy is in labor. Linda sits on the floor, giving Sandy's mother the only chair in the labor room. As Sandy dilates, they both help her with the contractions. "Her mother was at one leg, and I was at the other," Linda remembered after it was over. About 12:45 P.M., Sandy gives birth to a beautiful little girl. As the doctor tends to the teen, he asks Linda, "Now, why don't you hold your beautiful daughter?"

Hospital policy prohibits the adoptive parents from taking possession of their baby inside the hospital, so the next day they greet Sandy in the parking lot. She hands them the one-day-old child, wispy-haired and tightly swaddled. Linda remembers looking at her husband, with his sandy hair, then at the baby and thinking, "How odd, they look so much alike." Then she remembers hugging him.

Sandy did not back out, something adoptive parents fear most during private adoptions. Often teen mothers do decide to keep their babies, even after they have given the child to its adoptive parents. In Sandy's case, she wanted only the right to see pictures of the baby as she grew and to send Christmas and birthday presents. The Smiths hear from her occasionally and send her pictures and progress reports. Now, twenty-two months later, the adoption has been finalized.

The Smiths consider themselves lucky people who were "in the right place at the right time." Other arrangements often don't work out as well.

YOUNG BIRTH MOTHERS ARE KEEPING THEIR BABIES

Few young American women today are willing to relinquish the children they bear while unmarried. Many choose to keep their babies, collect welfare and live in their parents' homes. Times have changed dramatically since the days when single parents were ostracized by society.

One child we know who decided to keep her baby was even given a standing ovation by her high-school graduating class when she walked up, seven months pregnant, to receive her diploma. (It was an unusual accomplishment for a pregnant teen, since most do not finish high school.)

Peer pressure to keep these "love babies" is mounting, as is parental pressure. Some say Title IX, the law passed in 1972 that made it illegal to expel a pregnant student, has fueled this change in attitude.[22] Others point the finger at high-profile individuals, including prominent movie stars, who routinely have children without benefit of a marriage license. Still others say pregnant teens are afraid their children will, like little Lisa Steinberg in Queens, make front-page news as victims of child abuse.

It is often the young and poor women, the ones with few alternatives, who suffer the most from an unwanted pregnancy. Those who can afford it sometimes choose abortion, but even that may become an endangered procedure as militants fight to withhold abortion funding for low-income women and, ultimately, make abortion illegal.

Studies show, however, that the rolls of adoptable infants would not necessarily swell if abortions were outlawed. Unmarried women denied abortions only rarely give up their unwanted babies.

Knowing this, we have to ask ourselves what kinds of lives these babies have to look forward to. The *San Francisco Chronicle* reported that many of these women may harbor resentment and anger toward their children. In fact, children born to women who couldn't get an abortion

> are much likelier to be troubled and depressed, to drop out of school, to commit crimes, to suffer from serious illnesses and to express dissatisfaction with life, than are the offspring of willing parents.[23]

Consider these statistics:

More young women get pregnant every year. A survey by the *Ms.* Foundation for Women in 1991 found that every year more than one million young women between the ages of twelve and nineteen become pregnant.

Less than 3 percent of all babies born out of wedlock go to adoptive homes; 97 percent of all unmarried women opt to raise their own children.

These young women drop out of school for "family reasons" at rates double to triple that of young men.[24]

Adopted children are much less likely to live in poverty than children raised by unmarried mothers, and unmarried mothers who place their children for adoption are less likely to subsequently live in poverty, need public assistance, become pregnant again soon or resolve subsequent pregnancies by abortion.[25]

Teenage mothers who keep their babies are a major contributor to what has been called the "feminization of poverty" in the United States, and, according to the Ms. Foundation in late 1991, "their children comprise the single largest group of people in the United States living in poverty."[26]

CONCLUSIONS

More and more of these babies who stay with teenage mothers are relinquished when they get older. Experts have documented a pattern of teenage mothers who grow tired of the early responsibility and poverty and eventually relinquish the children they chose to keep as infants. They become the special-needs children who wait for adoptive families in foster care homes and residential centers.

The reality is that children do best when they are adopted before age two, yet more frequently they are relinquished once they are over five, have grown to mistrust adults and life in general and will be difficult to parent.

Ironically, couples who want newborns must wait four to five years for a child, while the thirty-five thousand children already on adoption roles—mostly older children in some way challenged—can expect to wait at least six years in foster care before they are matched with adoptive families.

The further reality is that both prospective families and children are available, and we must find a way to bring them together. Otherwise, society will suffer the consequences.

---

[1] National Committee for Adoption, *Adoption Factbook*, 1989, p. 157.

[2] Ibid., p. 96.

[3] Verna Noel Jones, "Delaying Childbirth: Researchers Work to Eliminate Dangers of Freezing Human Eggs," *Denver Rocky Mountain News*, October 12, 1990, p. 32.

[4] National Committee for Adoption, *Adoption Factbook*, p. 6.

[5] *Ms.* magazine, "Women as Wombs" (May/June 1991): pp. 28–35.

6 Ibid.

7 Kris Newcomer, "New Procedure Creates Ethical Dilemma, but GIFT of Life Often Last Chance for Couples," *Denver Rocky Mountain News,* October 7, 1990, p. 8.

8 Ibid.

9 *Washington Post,* January 26, 1988, p. 13.

10 National Committee for Adoption, *Adoption Factbook,* p.116.

11 Patti Foster, "Could You Have a Baby for Someone Else?" *For Women First* magazine (June 10, 1991): p. 128.

12 Ibid.

13 *Ms.* magazine, "Women as Wombs," p. 31.

14 *The Denver Post,* "Surrogate Contract Invalid, Judge Rules," October 23, 1990.

15 Kathy Stovall, *For Women First* magazine (June 1991): pp. 128–29.

16 Ibid.

17 Dixie van de Flier Davis, Rocky Mountain Adoption Exchange, personal interview, April 17, 1991.

18 Joel Williams, *Associated Press,* interview with Jeff Rosenberg, public policy director for the National Committee for Adoption, June, 1988.

19 *The Denver Post,* February 15, 1985, p. 6 .

20 *Denver Rocky Mountain News,* January 22, 1984, p. 23.

21 "Linda Smith," personal interview, 1990.

22 Elise F. Jones, et al.,*Teenage Pregnancy in Industrialized Countries,* 1986, pp. 37–38.

23 *San Francisco Chronicle,* May 19, 1991, p. 6.

24 The *Ms.* Foundation for Women, *National Girls Initiative,* August 20, 1991, p. 1.

25 National Committee for Adoption, *Adoption Factbook,* pp. 6–7.

26 The *Ms.* Foundation for Women, *National Girls Initiative,* p. 2.

CHAPTER THREE

FOSTER CARE SYSTEM PROBLEMS

There is something about a bureaucrat
that does not like a poem.
Gore Vidal,
Sex, Death and Money

"Melissa" was fifteen and settled into a comfortable foster home the first time we met her. She talked about the series of ups and downs that led her there, the stepfather who molested her at twelve, the two years on her own, then a stint in an abusive foster home that began at age fourteen. She ran away for awhile, then got lucky and landed in a good foster home. She talked about the hard years:

> I see kids going through a lot of problems, a lot of pain. You know, they're going into a foster home because they have problems. Then they get to the foster home and, if the family ain't a caring family ... it brings more emotional problems. I've seen the foster parents mistreat them. I've seen the real kids of the foster parents mistreat them. There is a lot of pain and suffering.

[These kids] are looking for somebody to make them feel special, make them feel like they're wanted, and you know, it's sad. By looking at them you can see they're hurting inside.

I've never found a place that I feel comfortable in. Most of the time they end up just not caring or mistreating me. The places I have been don't use the money for you. My aunt applied for foster care. She was getting money, and I never once seen not even a penny of it. It was not only myself, it was two other little girls, a five and a ten-year-old. They weren't being fed right. [The electric company] turned the lights out in the house, turned out the heat.

In the last foster home I was in, to me it seemed like they were just using the money for the house payment. There was a little baby. I think he was about eight months, a little baby. He was always left upstairs unattended, crying all day.

I would go upstairs and there he would be in the crib, the same place I'd seen him earlier that morning, crying and crying and crying and crying. ... Diaper wet. Blanket wrapped around his head. You don't know how that is going to affect a baby. You don't know how they're going to grow up.

You know, caseworkers say that a foster home is a good home, they're caring people. They'll give you what you need: clothes, food, a place to sleep. A lot of it isn't true. There's a lot of things that go on in a foster home.

Nobody knows what goes on behind closed doors. It's awful.[1]

Melissa became a ward of the state of California at age fourteen, although it wasn't her idea. "I never wanted to be a dependent of the court," she says. "The thought always scared me," but people told her that foster care was there to help, "like when you didn't have a family or needed a place. I turned to them," she says, "and it was a real bad experience."

"It's hard to find a foster home that's willing to take in teenagers. They hear the word teenager, and they get scared. But it's hard to find a good family, a really good family that's going to accept you and stand by you," Melissa says.

The reality is that foster kids get mistreated and run away, she says. Some start taking drugs, turn to prostitution, drop out of school. "Nothing's important to them no more."

"You know," she says, "we're just people, like everybody else, and we need the same love and attention that a little baby would need. But it's hard to find that ... especially if you're not blood-related."

The next time we talked to her, several months later, Melissa was floating again. The foster family she had been with decided they didn't have enough room in the house for her. Now sixteen, she had become legally emancipated, rented a room and gone to work full time. Melissa used to talk about the possibility of getting adopted someday, and thought it might have been a good thing. Now she sometimes, in her wildest dreams, thinks about what it would have been like to be adopted by her last foster parents, what it would have been like to feel secure, even if only for six or seven years.

Problems within the Child Welfare System

When challenged infants enter the child welfare system, they are greeted by a bureaucracy riddled with problems. Several areas need to be considered:

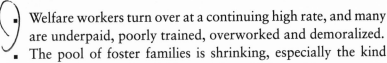

- Welfare workers turn over at a continuing high rate, and many are underpaid, poorly trained, overworked and demoralized.
- The pool of foster families is shrinking, especially the kind qualified to care for children with multiple problems.

- Services to prepare older youths in foster care for independent living are lacking.
- Permanent adoptive homes for older, handicapped and healthy minority children are in short supply.
- Needs of children in care are becoming increasingly complex and specialized, and there are few resources available to meet their needs.[2]

THE OLDER CHILD AND FOSTER CARE

On any given day in 1993, an estimated 600,000 American children are living apart from their biological parents, and more are on the way. In some states, the number of out-of-home placements is growing at the alarming rate of 20 percent a year, according to the New York-based Edna McConnell Clark Foundation.[3] The most conservative estimate, reported to the U.S. House of Representatives, predicts more than 840,000 children will be in out-of-home placements by the year 1995.[4] That includes children in the social service system placed in foster care or group homes as well as those in juvenile justice, mental health or special education facilities.

More than half of these children are away from their homes for a year or more. Three out of five live in more than one setting during their stay; some have fifteen or more "homes" before they leave the system. Many, like Melissa, will never live with a permanent family. The Foundation calls these children our country's youngest homeless. They are lost, the Foundation says, in a maze of programs and facilities, and once they are "lost in the system," they have little hope of being found.

About 60 percent of all children stalemated in temporary foster care situations and waiting for adoption are older children. Critics say most of them have been ruined by the system. After many placements in foster homes, with foster parents on guard against becoming "too attached," they learn not to love. They become what is clinically known as "attachment disordered," a condition that brings with it a long list of emotional and behavioral repercussions, many of which make the child almost impossible to parent.

Many of these children also have "fragile genetics." Dr. Foster Cline of Evergreen, Colorado, describes such children in the foster care system as coming from dysfunctional families and possessing a predisposition for such things as drug use, alcoholism and other challenges. Foster homes are called on to shelter them along with all the children who have lost their childhoods through abuse or neglect— babies who were stuffed into trash cans and left for dead, children who were beaten, burned, sexually molested, raped, abandoned or thrown out of the house. Such horrors are facts of life for thousands of American youngsters.

Across the board, placements of all kinds are increasing sharply. Many blame the increase on drug use and escalating poverty. The statistics are staggering:

- From 1985 to 1990, foster care rolls swelled from 47,700 to 78,900 children in California, a 65 percent increase that required 75 percent more funding.
- During the same time period, New York placements increased 115 percent, from 27,200 to 58,500.
- The number of children admitted to private psychiatric institutions rose nationally between 1980 and 1986 from 16,735 to 42,503, a 154 percent increase.

While drug use and poverty are factors in these epidemic placement numbers, Peter Forsythe of the Edna McConnell Clark Foundation also points the finger at "ignorance, inertia and insensitivity." He blames the government for overusing the foster care system when other solutions would work better.

"In this country, we remove too many children from their families, place them too far away, spend too much money doing so, and unnecessarily hurt children and parents in the process," he told the U.S. House of Representatives in 1991.[5]

He echoed the concern voiced by Congressman George Miller a year earlier. During a U.S. House Committee on Ways and Means hearing, Miller assessed the effectiveness of the Adoption Assistance and Child Welfare Act passed a decade earlier.

"Ten years after [its] passage, I'm sorry to say that the status of most of the children in the foster care system is as bad as it was when we started to reform the system," he said.[6]

Similar evidence was reported by the House Select Committee on Children, Youth and Families in 1989:

- The number of U.S. children in foster care (not including those in the justice system, mental institutions or special schools) rose an estimated 23 percent between 1985 and 1988 to more than 340,000 children, and it is predicted to reach 553,000 by 1995.
- No significant progress has been made in reducing the average length of stay of children in foster care. In 1985, for example, about 40 percent of children remained in care for more than two years.
- Forty-two percent of children who entered foster care in 1988 were under six years of age, up from 37 percent in 1985.
- The majority of children in foster care were white, although the number of minority children was increasing.[7]

Designed to be a short-term arrangement ending in either adoption or the child's return to a competent parent, foster care has become instead a kind of indeterminate sentence. Peter Forsythe calls it a system out of control, a place where we are "trading the *risk* of harm [from parents] with the *known* harm of removal" (italics added).

"We don't know if they will undergo harm at home, but we do know that removing them will cause problems. This knee-jerk response of yanking the kids out of the home isn't serving them very well."[8]

VULNERABILITY OF FOSTER CHILDREN

- The foster family is in the process of adopting the child but there has been some delay in the procedure.
- The child is the permanent ward of the agency.
- The child was raised in a violent environment.
- The child has special needs or a handicap.
- The child has been sexually abused.
- The child originally was placed into the foster care system because of maltreatment by birth parents.
- The child is an adolescent; particularly vulnerable are adolescents who've been previously abused.

Just as tragic, once children are in foster care, many who should be free for adoption are not. It is estimated that only 13 percent of the children currently in foster care are free for adoption.

"Only half of all foster children return home," according to *Time* magazine, "but many of the rest are suspended in a legal limbo by parents who make little effort to regain their children, but refuse to relinquish them fully."[9]

Dr. Vera Fahlberg, a Seattle, Washington, pediatrician who is one of the country's leading advocates for children, has done extensive writing about the attachment and separation issues such children face. "Loss is never completely resolved," she says, "It may recycle in a variety of ways."[10]

Peter Forsythe says it is better to place children with relatives than with complete strangers, because "the shock of placement for some children is reduced and the degree of estrangement from the biological family [is] minimized." Unfortunately, the existing foster care system is designed to discourage such placements.

Children placed in relatives' homes spend more time there than those placed in regular foster care homes, and as their stay increases, so does the cost. "If children living with paid relatives becomes the dominant form of foster care," says Forsythe, "and if these children stay longer and essentially grow up with relatives, the average length of stay in foster care could easily more than double."[11] The costs would follow suit.

ROSA

Relatives tried to raise fourteen-year-old Rosa after she was taken from her mother's home, but her problems were too difficult for them to handle. Rosa was born to an alcoholic mother and was exposed to alcohol *in utero*. Hundreds of thousands of drug- and alcohol-exposed children are born each year in America.

Like the estimated 375,000 children each year exposed before birth to drugs or alcohol in America, she pays the price in developmental delays and a low IQ.[12] To illustrate the problem of drug and alcohol abuse and its effect on children, it is important to know that more than 4.5 million women of childbearing age were current users of illegal drugs in 1990. Only 14 percent of women needing drug treatment receive it.[13]

At the tender age of six, Rosa was making all the decisions in the home—when to eat, what to do, how to dress. This half-white, half-Native American child found her own way to school on the few days she could manage it. As time went on, the little girl became her mother's mother, taking care of the hung-over woman, telling her what to do and feeding her.

Rosa finally was removed from the home and bounced from one relative to another as the beleaguered foster care system tried to find her a more permanent home. It wasn't easy to place such a troubled teen, and since no one was there to guide her, she took a wrong turn. Rosa now is a gang leader's moll, hanging out with the "bad" kids, stealing, smoking, sleeping around and doing drugs. As of this printing, Rosa was expecting her own child, and no one knew if the baby would be impaired. Because Rosa is a "throw-away" child, no one seemed to care, either.

THE INFANT IMPACT

Infants such as Rosa's are impacting the foster care system in ways that were previously unimaginable. Consider the following:

- Unprecedented numbers of children ages birth to four years entered the system in the late '80s and early '90s.
- Infants and toddlers affected by maternal drug use and alcohol abuse during pregnancy and babies born with HIV are providing an already overwhelmed system with new challenges.
- Prenatal programs that might identify risks early on are inaccessible and inadequate, further complicating the situation.[14]

Perhaps the most frightening repercussion of these trends is the long-term picture. When infants born with challenges—drug exposure, alcohol exposure, HIV, developmental delays, physical disabilities—enter the system, they are usually there for good. They bounce from one foster home to the next, getting more disconnected each time they are moved. By age two, some are virtually destroyed. Finding adoptive homes for them is nearly impossible.

Foster Home Abuse

As much as officials would like to deny it, Melissa is not the only child who has encountered abusive foster parents. A 1984 study funded by the National Center on Child Abuse and Neglect found that thirty claims of abuse were substantiated for every one thousand children in foster care.[15] Because states lack consistent reporting and tracking methods, only twenty-seven states and 137,389 foster families were included in that study.

Although the numbers of abused children are small, it's ironic that *any* children are being abused in the system set up to protect them. Some experts believe the foster care system drives families to abuse by pushing them beyond their breaking points. Such families are seen as successful by agencies that may unwittingly overload them by giving them the most difficult children. Agencies also:

- Make emergency placements;
- Overload foster homes, sending more children than they can reasonably handle;
- Fail to match the foster child with the family's preferences and abilities;
- Fail to visit the homes or provide foster parent training.

In some cases, the children themselves can make the situation worse. Although children should never be held responsible for their own mistreatment, abused foster children share characteristics that can make them particularly challenging and vulnerable. Studies have found that episodes of abuse generally stem from "attempts to control behavior that appears to the foster parents to be bizarre, dangerous, difficult or defiant."[16]

A needy child's behavior may drive foster parents away with incidents of fecal smearing, soiling or verbal challenges. Foster parents who are not adequately prepared will find such behaviors strange, confusing and the source of a never-ending struggle for control.

Despite these instances, it should be pointed out that good foster care families are the rule rather than the exception, offering first-rate environments that nurture their small wards and clearly have the children's interests at heart. These special parents work with the children, transport them to appointments and visits with their parents and generally provide them with love, structure and care.

Kimm and Greg Bolding of Colorado are just such foster parents, caring for seven children. Kimm has even gone to the length of breast-feeding her latest charge, a very ill infant born drug-exposed.

FISCAL CONSIDERATIONS

It is impossible to understand the burgeoning out-of-home placement rates without understanding the fiscal incentives supporting this trend. The costs of out-of-home care generally are divided among city, state and federal governments. "Under current law, states receive significantly more federal funds to maintain children in foster care than to provide preventive services that can reduce the need for out-of-home placements," states the most recent summary of information on America's children and their families compiled by the National Commission on Children.[17] It's not surprising that financially strapped state and city officials are inclined to choose foster care.

California is probably the worst-case scenario. The state government pays 95 percent of the costs of keeping a child in foster care, but none of the cost of services to the birth family if the child is not removed. County governments must pick up the entire tab for such preventative services.

"This means that the in-home services must be twenty times cheaper before they are 'worth it' to the county," says Peter Forsythe. "Guess which state has the highest out-of-home population in the country, a population that also is growing at one of the most rapid rates?" California, of course.

"Don't let anyone tell you that the correlation between fiscal incentives and out-of-home placement is an accident."[18]

When adjusted for inflation, the spending on preventative services scarcely grew over the past decade; but spending on out-of-home care more than tripled. The open-ended entitlement grew from about $467 million in 1981 to more than $1.76 billion in 1991.[19]

Such "open-ended" appropriations for out-of-home care provide another financial incentive for foster care. If funds for foster care run out midyear, the state government usually feels it has no choice but to supplement the budget. There are hungry mouths to feed, after all. When money for preventative services runs out, it is usually impossible to get more.

Yet when the cost per case is compared, it can be very cost-effective to keep children in their own homes. In fact, family preservation services are almost always more cost-effective than foster care. For example, the median cost of supporting one child in family foster care for one year is $17,500, nearly six times the median cost of providing family preservation services ($3,000 per child).

Consider these 1991 per-child averages from the state of Washington, based on a yearly cost:

- Family preservation, $2,800;
- Foster family placement, $4,500;
- Group placement, $22,400;
- An episode of acute psychiatric hospitalization, $45,000;
- Long-term psychiatric treatment, $103,000.[20]

As President Bill Clinton prepared to pledge $2.3 billion to foster care in 1993, critics charged that pumping more money into the existing system is not the answer.

Some Potential Solutions

Solutions must start at the beginning, which means that assessment of the needs of at-risk children must start even before they are born. Good prenatal care is both cost-effective and preventative in nature. If a woman at risk for a low-birth-weight delivery receives early and frequent prenatal exams, the U.S. health care system can save between $14,000 and $30,000 in short- and long-term costs.[21] Drug and alcohol treatment for pregnant women also could alleviate the extent to which their babies suffer the effects of drug and alcohol exposure *in utero*.

A variety of other imaginative, red-tape-cutting programs are needed if the child welfare system is to deal with the deluge of children coming its way. Some critics say that the entire foster care budget should be turned over to programs that focus on family preservation and adoption services instead. Michigan, New York and Connecticut already channel their foster care money into family preservation programs.

A less drastic approach in Detroit, called Living in Family Environments (L.I.F.E.), has received national attention for bringing together two disenfranchised groups: welfare families and handicapped children. It serves only fourteen special-needs children but is noteworthy for its imaginative approach to old problems.

Families on public assistance are recruited and trained to care for foster children between ten and eighteen who are physically or mentally handicapped and would otherwise live in institutions. Their salaries—$22,000 a year plus medical benefits—enable the families to get off welfare. Training includes classes in managing developmental difficulties, home management, health and safety, nutrition, hygiene, communication and use of community resources. Each family must attend monthly in-service trainings, and each has access to respite care, which allows the family an occasional break from the child.

Washington and Idaho have reduced social workers' caseloads to ten children each so they can deliver intensive services to parents and, if that fails, recruit foster parents interested in adopting the children. They have successfully reduced a child's average wait for a permanent family to thirteen months, with 82 percent of the children being in only one foster home during that time.

Former Texas Senator Lloyd Bentsen also introduced a bill during the first days of the 102nd Congress that could have a significant impact on families and the child welfare system, if passed. Among other things, it calls for:

- Enabling states to plan, develop or expand innovative programs to preserve and strengthen families and prevent the need for foster care placement;
- Providing new family preservation, reunification, follow-up and respite care services to adoptive families as well as biological families ($1.65 billion over five years);

- Requiring periodic case review of all children legally free for adoption, providing adoption assistance funds and providing a one-time tax deduction of up to $3,000 for adopting a special-needs child;
- Promoting drug and alcohol abuse prevention programs for pregnant women and mothers with children, to include drug and alcohol treatment, prenatal and pediatric medical, home visitation, child care and parenting education.

Innovative family preservation programs could be successful 50 percent of the time, supporters estimate. If that's the case, and we can save half the youngsters now going into out-of-home placement, the system can then focus all of its resources and attention on the special needs of the remaining 50 percent.

Conclusions

Why are American children being discarded at record rates and what can we do to help? There are many deep-rooted problems that will require the efforts of all segments of society and will include changing the parenting techniques of thousands of people, treating drug abuse and stemming the cycle of abuse. The task may seem overwhelming, but we must act if we are to save the thousands of abandoned and discarded children.

We must act quickly so that the future of an entire generation of children does not slip away. These are problems that can be solved. Already, there are many solutions to the problems of our unwanted children. It is clear that we are putting our money in the wrong places. But while we are waiting to redirect foster care money to the adoption arena, there are smaller things we can do.

Action is needed, not tomorrow, but now.

---

[1] "Melissa," personal interview, Los Angeles, California, June 1991.

[2] Edna McConnell Clark Foundation, 1991.

[3] Edna McConnell Clark Foundation, *Keeping Families Together: Facts on Family Preservation Services*, June 1993.

[4] U.S. House Select Committee on Children, Youth and Families, "No Place to Call Home: Discarded Children in America," December 11, 1989.

[5] Peter W. Forsythe, testimony, U.S. House Subcommittee on Children, Family, Drugs and Alcoholism, Committee on Labor and Human Resources, Feb. 20, 1991.

[6] Congressman George Miller, testimony, Subcommittee on Human Resources of the U.S. House Committee on Ways and Means, April, 1990, reported in *Adoptalk*, Spring 1990, p. 2.

[7] U.S. House Select Committee, "No Place to Call Home."

[8] Peter Forsythe, director Edna McConnell Clark Foundation, personal interview, 1991.

[9] *Time* magazine (October 9, 1989): p. 87.

[10] North American Council on Adoptable Children annual conference, 1991, Atlanta, Georgia.

[11] Peter Forsythe of the Edna McConnell Clark Foundation, personal communication, April 1991.

[12] National Commission on Children, *Just the Facts: A Summary of Recent Information on America's Children and Their Families*, Washington, DC, 1993, p. 65.

[13] Children's Defense Fund, *The State of America's Children*, Washington, DC, 1992, p. 62.

[14] North American Council on Adoptable Children, *Challenges to Child Welfare*, November 1990, p. 3.

[15] McFadden and Ryan, "Abuse in Family Foster Homes: Characteristics of the Vulnerable Child" (paper presented at the Sixth International Congress on Child Abuse and Neglect, Sydney, Australia, August 1986).

[16] Ibid.

[17] National Commission on Children, *Just the Facts,* p. 155.

[18] Peter Forsythe, director Edna McConnell Clark Foundation, personal interview, 1991.

[19] National Commission on Children, *Just the Facts,* p. 155.

[20] Edna McConnell Clark Foundation, 1991.

[21] Report to the Chairman, Senate Committee on Finance, 1990, p. 38.

CHAPTER FOUR

ADOPTIVE SYSTEM PROBLEMS

Happy families are all alike;
every unhappy family is unhappy in its own way.
Leo Tolstoy,
Anna Karenina

Her name, she insists politely, is Lizbeth. She once knew a girl named Becky, but she is happy that Becky is now "off my back for good," she says.

Becky was not nice. She threw temper fits; cut up clothes, bed sheets and draperies; urinated in public and lashed out at those around her. She was "stuck in a rageful place" and refused to love anyone.

Lizbeth was that girl, but since she has been successfully treated for an attachment disorder, she feels like a different person. She and her adoptive parents washed the slate clean by legally changing her name. Instead of the adopted girl Becky, she is Lizbeth, like her great aunt, and with an "L" name like her two sisters.

It took a year in a therapeutic foster family facility for Lizbeth to come to terms with the abuse she suffered as a young child in her birth home. By the time she was removed from that home and put in the foster care system, she was unable to attach emotionally. Her bizarre and destructive behavior ended one home placement after another, but she got no therapy for her rage until after she was adopted.

As her adoptive mother says, "Now there is a new girl in there. Why, her eyes just sparkle. It is wonderful."[1]

Lizbeth's story is not unusual. According to a 1984 study, for every one thousand children in foster care, thirty were abused.[2] Lizbeth, also, is not the only one to have multiple moves in foster care; of the children in stubstitute care in 1988, almost 48 percent had experienced between two and five placements in the preceding three years, and 6.5 percent had six or more placements.[3] Each time they are moved, it is traumatic, even if the move is into an adoptive home. Even that doesn't guarantee an end to the problems. As adoption expert Kathryn Donley told the North American Council on Adoptable Children at its 1990 convention, "Adoption does not cure traumatized kids."

In fact, adoption can further traumatize them if it isn't done well. America's adoption system works too slowly for most children, leaving them in foster care long after they are ready for a permanent family. And once they are matched with adoptive parents, the system does little to help them adjust to each other. An estimated 13 percent of all adoptions fail—12 percent before the process is final and another 1 percent afterwards—because the parents and children aren't given the financial help and the mental health treatment they need. Each failure leaves the children a little more scarred.

When a child is given up—effectively *divorced*—after the adoption is final, the phenomenon is called *disillusionment*. As can be imagined, it is painful for the child and the parents. Some children are adopted and given back as many as three times before the system stops trying to place them. Most people wouldn't think of divorcing their birth children, no matter how bad the problems are, but adopted children often are viewed differently. Some parents get so distraught that they give up, especially in the teenage years. Although there is no data on disillusionment, experts believe it happens in 1–2 percent of all adoptions.

More commonly, families give back their adoptive children before the adoption has become final, a process called *disruption*. Experts believe this happens in 10–15 percent of the children's first adoptions, a process that can leave the children scarred and the adoptive parents feeling lifelong guilt.[4]

Such definitive information on adoption success rates comes from Richard P. Barth, who studied the problem in 1988 in *Adoption and Disruption: Rates, Risks and Responses.* He found that about 12 percent of all adoptions end in disruption before they become final. (This figure doesn't include children returned after their adoptions became final.) Disruption rates are much lower—only 1 percent—for children adopted before age two. Children most likely to be returned to their agencies are those between six and nineteen years old who have special needs. Some estimate these children's adoptions are disrupted 35 percent of the time, although others estimate as high as 75 percent. Unfortunately, they comprise the majority of the children now waiting for homes.

Sometimes the problems are financial. Children who need long-term psychological or residential treatment can run up bills of between $40,000 and $50,000 a year, pricing some adoptive parents out of the market. When the costs of treating a child's psychological illness get in the way of the adoption, it is called a *forced disillusionment.*

That's not to say that older, more difficult children can not be successfully adopted. Many success stories, including that of Lizbeth, are living proof that problems can be overcome. But experts agree that adoptive parents must be handpicked to fit the child's needs, know the risks from the very beginning and have help preparing for the challenge.

Special-needs children require parents who:

- Are loving and responsive, can provide consistent discipline and can deal with the child's fear, uncertainty and rejecting behavior;
- Have enough pre- and postadoption placement counseling to be prepared for the problems that will arise;
- Can understand and relate to the sort of problem this child will likely bring with him.

That may mean the best parents for special-needs children are those who already have experience raising children. "It doesn't always

follow that the Yuppie infertile baby boomer couple is the best resource," says Dixie van de Flier Davis, director of the Rocky Mountain Adoption Exchange.

The Troubled Adoption System

As we look closer at the difficulties of adoption, we get a clearer
picture of the many problems troubling America's adoption system:

1. Adoptive homes are limited.
2. The needs of today's foster children are making it more difficult to find them adoptive homes (especially the very challenged or drug-abused babies).
3. Adoption placements are often delayed for years for a variety of reasons.[5]

The system as it has been set up is a slow and sluggish one in
which money determines the fate of children. Some children are kept
in foster homes for years, primarily because money is available to care
for them there, but isn't available to help them in their birth homes or
in adoptive homes.

Foster care is financed by tax money because the average person
considers it his collective responsibility to protect children from
abusive or negligent parents. Adoption, on the other hand, is financed with a combination of private and public funds. It is harder to
convince the average taxpayer that it is his duty to provide the child
with a permanent adoptive home or to provide the child's birth parents with preventative therapy. As more drug-exposed babies and challenged children enter the foster care system and drain its resources,
the entire foster care/adoption system may begin to be viewed as a
whole.

Once children enter the foster care system, they often get bogged
down in the bureaucracy. In some cases, no future plans for adoption
or reunification with birth parents are drawn up, although they should
be. These children live out their young lives bouncing from one foster
home to another until, as angry teenagers, they run away or, as young
adults, they move out and try to survive on their own.

Even when adoption is identified as the goal for a child, it can take years to accomplish says the congressional report, "No Place to Call Home: Displaced Children in America." For example, the average child in Maryland in 1990 spent five years in foster care to be adopted. Children in New York wait an average of six years, even though the state's Child Welfare Reform Act prescribes a maximum wait of four years.[6]

The problem is not finding families, including minority families, according to the congressional report. The major problem "is getting these families through the system."

Even adoptive families prepared for the delays drop out during the process. One in four withdrew during the home study process in 1990, according to the report by the House Select Committee on Children, Youth and Families. The home study process should take a few weeks but instead can stretch to between six to nine months.[7] Efforts to locate permanent adoptive homes also have suffered as efforts have been refocused on "developing new foster care options and efforts to cope with the rising numbers in protective services."[8]

Also, adoption workers sometimes make serious mistakes with special-needs groups, experts claim. Early recognition and treatment of potential psychological problems can save a lot of trauma in later years, yet money for therapy is scarce. The foster care/adoption system often requires that sibling groups be adopted together, which often isn't necessary and which makes it extremely difficult to place the children. Some of these siblings have never lived together and may not even know each other. In other cases, one child may be attachment disordered and may delay the other healthy child's placement.

Another problem is children who are not free for adoption. Although children in foster care represent the largest group in out-of-home placement, many are not free for adoption for a variety of reasons. Some stay in foster care for years and are freed for adoption only after they become almost too old to adopt. They learn tragically that their age stands between them and the real family they have been waiting to join. Others become psychotic or unadoptable because they endure continued losses in a system supposedly designed to rescue them.[9]

Between 85 and 90 percent of the children seen at Connell Watkins and Associates in Evergreen, Colorado, are placed there by adoptive families on the verge of returning them to their agencies. If the intensive therapy provided by Connell Watkins doesn't work, Watkins says, these children often have no other choice than living in an institution.

Those in Congress who are working to change the system express frustration and anger at the lack of progress. Rep. Patricia Schroeder (D-Colorado), the senior female member of Congress, noted that the average adoption costs between $5,000 and $10,000, enough to keep many good potential parents out of the system. She is working on legislation that would require insurance companies to cover the cost of infertility treatments and of adoption.

The Costs

Private agency members of the National Committee for Adoptions report an average adoption fee of about $7,500, with costs ranging from a low of $900–$1,500 for public agencies to as high as $12,000 for adoptions from individuals or private agencies.[10] Foreign adoptions can require as much as $25,000, and some black market adoptions have commanded as much as $50,000 for infants.

Does all this amount to baby-buying? The more flagrant black market transactions certainly fit the description, but in some ways, so does the current legal adoption setup. "Fees are the single greatest barrier for minority families adopting minority children," says Dixie van de Flier Davis of the Rocky Mountain Adoption Exchange, and minority children now account for half the children in the foster care system.

Davis is lobbying to do away with adoption fees. She thinks it is absurd to make parents pay for the chance to adopt special-needs children, then ask them to pay for necessary remedial care or therapy, on top of requiring them to invest the rest of their lives in raising the child. She suggests a different approach—using the money now spent on foster care to subsidize adoptions. The 1992 U.S. budget for adoption is $201 million, less than 10 percent of the $2.3 billion foster care budget.

Instead of spending that money to keep children in foster homes and residential treatment, Davis would like to see it used to place children in permanent homes and to subsidize their mental health and medical care. Savings should be substantial, since costs of keeping kids in foster care go up as they get older.

"They go into more and more restrictive settings, not less," says Davis. She estimates the cost for residential treat most restrictive of all, at about $25,000 a month, a tab picked ˻ᵣ the foster care system.

Davis says her agency intends to promote the idea more aggressively in the next few years, and she hopes to find a legislator willing to introduce the concept to Congress as a solution to the foster care/ adoption crisis.

Stories like those of Shaneen and Connie, both children whose expensive therapy has interfered with their adoptions, illustrate the predicament.

SHANEEN

Years of bouncing around from one place to the next took their toll on six-year-old Shaneen, a mulatto child born to a woman thought to be schizophrenic. She lived with one acquaintance after another, lived on the streets and then moved into an institutionalized day treatment facility before Kimm and Gregory Bolding took her in.

The child they saved had been diagnosed as mentally ill and was headed for a residential institution when the Boldings found her. She has done well in their foster care, but the couple now desperately wants to adopt Shaneen. The only thing standing in their way is her mental health bills.

As long as Shaneen is a ward of the state's social services system, she has access to free treatment. If the Boldings adopt her, they will be required to pay for the lion's share of her therapy. And Shaneen has a number of problems that require expensive treatment.

"You name it, Shaneen has it," Kimm says. "She has been diagnosed as having just about every mental illness possible—dissociative behaviors; psychologically induced illnesses like fever, seizures, nose bleeds and pink eye; posttraumatic stress syndrome; major depression; sensory integration disorder; attention deficit hyperactivity; and oppositional defiant disorder." She may also be schizophrenic and dyslexic, and may have a number of developmental disorders.[11] The one thing she doesn't suffer from is attachment disorder.

"I think she was too mentally ill to get unattached when she was moved around," Kimm says. "For a long time [Shaneen] was heavily sedated, completely drugged out." In fact, the Boldings took her out of one day-care center that kept her heavily medicated and enrolled her full time in public school.

"Our caseworker says we literally have saved her life, as she has been very suicidal in the past," Kimm says.

Because of Shaneen's problems, the family was forced to start all over with nothing. The girl "accidently" burned down the last rented home they were in. "It was a mistake any child could have made," Kimm says, "but we couldn't get one bit of help from social services, not a toothbrush or anything." Now the homeowners' insurance company is suing the Boldings for damages. Even so, the couple wants nothing more than to make Shaneen a permanent part of their family.

"The day treatment worker asked why we would want a kid like her," Kimm says. Her answer: "I'm furious that you can't see the beauty in my child. Why, we adore her."

By first becoming Shaneen's foster parents and then declaring their intention to adopt (in essence, becoming Fos/Adopt parents), the Boldings took the first step in the adoption process. In many states, this is called the "legal risk program," which means the adopting family acts as foster parents until the child is relinquished by its birth parents or until the details of subsidies can be worked out to the satisfaction of all. Unfortunately, the money for extensive therapy often isn't there.

As of spring 1994, the Boldings hadn't been able to finalize the adoption. "We just can't afford to do it and take the risk of not getting financial help for mental health treatments," Kimm says.

Shaneen's story is not unique. Many children who are emotionally ill remain in the custody of the state because there isn't enough money for treatment.

CONNIE

Dianne Allred, a single woman living in Utah, didn't know what she was in for when she decided to adopt "Connie." The child has severe attachment disorders and a personality her therapist describes as "like Swiss cheese," the result of an early childhood marred by multiple incidences of abuse. Allred felt that Connie deserved a chance, and thought she might be that chance.

"I felt I could help her," Allred says. "After all, she was only six. You can't give up on a little child like that."

Allred didn't count on adopting a child so disturbed she needed round-the-clock supervision. She found out she couldn't provide the necessary time and structure and still make a living. She wound up sending Connie to an expensive, structured full-time residential treatment family, paid for by the Utah Department of Social Services. The payments will continue only until the day Allred signs the finalization papers on Connie's adoption.

"It appears now that I may not be able to finalize the adoption," her mother sighs. "But I'll always be committed to Connie, all her life. I don't want her to think I abandoned her, just like all the others. I may not be able to be her mother, but I can be her advocate."

Each six months, Allred must go before a judge to have her guardianship extended so Connie's treatment bills will be picked up the state. The experience has been so painful the forty-year-old woman isn't sure if she will ever attempt another adoption.

"Right now, I'm looking into artificial insemination," Allred says. "That may be the best route for me to get a child."

Changing the Requirements

The best families to care for special-needs children may not fit the present adoption requirements. Critics of the system say the old criteria for choosing prospective parents are arbitrary and not applicable to today's children awaiting adoption.

For example, in agency adoptions, the standards for adoptive parents can vary widely, depending on the types of children they place. Usually, agencies want to know:

- How long have you been married? (Most prefer two or three years.)
- How old are you? (Most place babies with people between twenty-one and forty years old.)
- What sort of child are you looking for?

These are reasonable questions, but birth parents of teenagers are older than most parents of infants. Why shouldn't people in their 40s and 50s be allowed to adopt teenagers? A more realistic measure of the ability to parent might include such things as:

- Emotional maturity, including the ability to solve problems and adjust expectations (previous parenting experience can be helpful). Older couples should not be disqualified, especially if they have raised children with special needs.
- A stable marital relationship. This will screen out parents who are trying to adopt to "save the marriage."
- A strong desire to be a parent. Other helpful qualities are patience, flexibility and the ability to tolerate stress.

Those couples parenting special-needs children also need a sense of humor, says Virginia Appel of the Rocky Mountain Adoption Exchange, and must be willing to make an unconditional, lifelong commitment to a child who may not attach to them for months or years. "They also should have a good support network of family and friends and be willing to seek and accept help if necessary, including long-term therapy."[12]

Once couples have passed those tests, a personality assessment should be done to help the agency match them with a child of similar temperament.

Federal Help for Adoptive Parents

In early 1993, the adoptive family got a boost from the federal government. The Family Leave Bill became law, requiring unpaid, job-protected leaves of absence for parents following the adoption of a child. It also allows parents to take time off to care for an ill child or elderly parent.

The new law will help with the transition and bonding period in adoption, when many of these issues are confronted. Rep. Patricia Schroeder introduced the bill several sessions earlier, having taken the stand that families should not be barred from adoption just because both parents must work.

It is the authors' opinion that couples who adopt should commit to having at least one care giver at home to bond with the child. This can be either the mother or father, or another caring adult such as a grandparent or nanny. The key is consistency. Whoever the child bonds with should be available to the child over the long haul.

Conclusions

In conclusion, it is the responsibility of adoptive parents to insist that agencies provide the following before placement of a child:

1. Full disclosure of the child's background and history;
2. Disclosure of any physical or mental problems that could be genetic in origin. This could involve hiring a geneticist to do an evaluation;
3. A complete report on current and past psychological tests and evaluations;
4. Personality and temperament testing of family and child (see sample of the Stevens Adopt-Match Evaluator in Appendix II);
5. In-depth preadoptive parenting classes (get the agreement in writing);
6. Aid with any future therapy costs for the adopted child, should they be necessary; and
7. A plan for intensive follow-up services after the adoption, so-called "postadoption services."

The authors would also like to emphasize that caseworkers handling adoption cases also have responsibilities, including:

1. Doing a thorough investigation of the child's background, even when the birth parents are unwilling participants;
2. Preparing a complete Life Book for the child covering all aspects of life from day one;
3. Making sure the adoptive parents are compatible with the child and will be capable of handling future problems;
4. Making sure the adoptive parents can provide a safe, loving,

consistent environment and can help the child through the grieving process;

5. Supporting the adoptive family after the adoption;
6. Arranging visits to observe the ways family members interact. This is the easiest way to detect problems between the child and family before they "go underground" or escalate into a crisis;
7. Providing adequate and thorough training for adoptive parents, including caveats about problems; and
8. Making sure adoptive parents with high-risk children listen to warnings about potential problems. They should be warned before the placement and no less than three other times.

It is in the area of mental health care for children that adoptive parents need the most help. As statistics become available, it is clear that many children available for adoption have mental health issues. National Adoption Center statistics show that 52 percent of all children waiting for adoption have some kind of emotional problems. U.S. Department of Education figures show that in 1990, only one in five children who needed help actually got it.[13]

After reviewing the Adoption Assistance and Child Welfare Act of 1980, Public Law 96-272, the authors also believe that it is mandatory that Congress enforce the intent of the legislation, which requires that:

> Agencies make reasonable efforts to prevent unnecessary placement of children outside their homes, to reunite children with their biological families and to find permanent adoptive homes for children who can not return home.

The authors add that it should be mandatory to find these adoptive homes as fast as is humanly possible. Psychologists and psychiatrists are just beginning to realize the crisis that can occur when children fail to attach to a person of trust during childhood. Research has shown that all children need at least one connection with one person during their early childhood to survive and thrive.

That person can be a parent, a member of a foster family, a long-term therapist or an adoptive parent.

The authors have seen children of all ages survive through chaos when they have had only one long-term relationship with a therapist or teacher. Depriving them of a long-term relationship can cause severe damage to the children. And even children who enter the foster care system with severe behavior problems fare better when they are identified and treated early in the process.

We must provide children with permanent families, for "children are too precious a natural resource for our nation to disregard."[14]

Although the Child Welfare Act has been on the books for years, progress has been very slow. Agencies mandated to make explicit treatment plans for families in crisis have failed to do so. Many believe that removing a child from a troubled family is the best or only way to ensure safety, disregarding the negative impact such a drastic move has on the child. Peter Forsythe of the Edna McConnell Clark Foundation outlines two common consequences:

- The guilt of children who misunderstand and assume they are to blame for their family's disintegration;
- The pain of being summarily removed from all that is familiar and being deposited in a strange house with strange people, beds, smells, foods, schools, rules, neighbors and sometimes even language.

Then, add more shock and fear than most of us have ever had to experience, says Forsythe.[15]

Whenever a child *must* be removed from the home of origin for safety reasons, a permanency plan must be developed immediately so the child does not languish in the system. To make this happen, the authors suggest the following:

- Foster care and adoption agencies must work in concert in determining the best possible permanent placement, using temperament tests to determine whether relatives or strangers will make the best adoptive parents.

- If the agency rules that the parents and child can be helped through counseling, that alternative should be pursued.
- If the family of origin is legally judged to be abusive or negligent, and the child is judged to be unsafe with them, immediate relinquishment proceedings must be started to sever the child's attachments with the abusive or negligent family and to place the child's name on a national adoption register.
- An adoptive family must be sought to meet the needs of the child.
- That adoptive family must be given full disclosure of the child's history and must know the consequences of that history.
- The new parents must get financial help to pay for therapy the child likely will need to deal with the new situation.
- Extensive pre- and postadoption counseling must be done with the child and the family to make sure the adoption is working and the child is being assimilated into the family.

If all of the above procedures are done, the authors are convinced the child and the adoptive family will have every opportunity to function as a family. The alternative is to allow the staggering loss and grief of the current system to continue.

Adopted children, certainly, suffer from emotional disorders. But the number of children receiving adequate treatment is minuscule.

ADOPTIVE FAMILIES ARE THE CURE

The new adoptive family should not be the source of the problem, but the source of a cure. The truth is that adopting a child with a history of abuse, a physical or mental handicap or born exposed to drugs or HIV can be extremely difficult. But those who do reach out to these vulnerable children can also find it to be deeply rewarding.

---

[1] Attachment Center at Evergreen, Colorado, "Kansas City: Unattached Becky and Angie," videotape, 1990.

[2] Edna McConnell Clark Foundation, *Keeping Families Together: Facts on Family Preservation Services*, "Lost in the System," 1991.

[3] National Commission on Children, *Just the Facts: A Summary of Recent Information on America's Children and Their Families*, Washington DC, 1993, p. 156.

[4] Richard P. Barth, *Adoption and Disruption: Rates, Risks and Responses*, 1988.

[5] U.S. House Select Committee on Children, Youth and Families, "No Place to Call Home: Discarded Children in America," December 11, 1989.

[6] The Foster Care Monitoring Committee's Report to the Mayor of New York, 1990.

[7] U.S. House Select Committee, "No Place to Call Home."

[8] Ibid.

[9] Ken Magid and Carole McKelvey, *High Risk: Children without a Conscience* (New York: Bantam, 1988).

[10] Scripps Howard News Service, January 1987.

[11] Kimm Bolding, personal interview, Colorado Springs, Colorado, January 1990.

[12] Virginia Appel, Boulder Adoption Fair speech, Fall 1990, Boulder, Colorado.

[13] U.S. Department of Education, 1990.

[14] Peter Forsythe of the Edna McConnell Clark Foundation, personal interview, New York, Summer 1990.

[15] Ibid.

SPECIAL PROBLEMS

CHAPTER FIVE

HALF-TRUTHS AND LAWSUITS

> *Monday's Child is fair of face,*
> *Tuesday's Child is full of grace,*
> *Wednesday's child is full of woe ...*
>   A. Bray (1838),
>   *Traditions of Devone*

Wednesday's Child

The camera catches sweet, blond, cherubic Barbara at the Fort Worth Zoo. The twelve-year-old, dressed in pink shorts and white straw sandals, pets baby deer and rabbits for the camera. She is in the market for adoptive parents, and she is on her best behavior.

When Barbara's story airs on Channel 8 in Dallas, Texas, anchor John Criswell tells viewers "that up until now Barbara's life has been one of terror. Barbara was severely victimized, and it will always affect her life."[1] He doesn't say that until a few months earlier, Barbara was a prostitute known on Dallas streets as "Raspberry."

Barbara's first sexual experiences came as a child, when she was given to her mother's boyfriends as a sexual present. Her mother was schizophrenic, her father an alcoholic. Later Barbara hit the streets, turning tricks for a pimp named Star Child. When she fled from him and asked local police for protection, she bore little resemblance to the angelic pink girl visiting the zoo. She wore hooker-style makeup, spiked hair and a black miniskirt.

Since she turned herself in, Barbara has been living in a state-licensed group home, taking medications for depression and anxiety. But that bit of information isn't included in the two-minute television segment. Instead, the anchorman says she is a good student and "a survivor." A phone number flashes on the screen as he says, "Now she needs parents to help her thrive."

Barbara is the kind of severely abused child who may never respond to an adoptive family. Her problems may be more than any one family can cope with, especially a family unprepared for trauma. Like others featured in "Wednesday's Child" segments, Barbara comes with a lot of history.

"The 'Wednesday's Child' up for adoption on TV may be the answer to your prayers," wrote journalist Jan Jarboe in *Texas Monthly.* "Then again, the darling you take home may be a ticking time bomb, a former ward of the state so abused and so volatile that your family will never know what hit it."[2]

Most of the children featured on the program are abandoned by their birth parents and have been abused so severely that their lives were at stake before entering the child welfare system. The federal government does not keep statistics on adoption and the circumstances of the children up for adoption, but in 1988 almost half (46.9 percent) of out-of-home placements were for children needing protection from adults in their own homes.[3] Each week since the mid-1970s, however, public service programs around the country have featured their woeful faces.

The "Wednesday's Child" concept started in Texas, where it evolved from pet-of-the-week features. It turned out to be a powerful weapon in recruiting parents for hard to place children, and was duplicated in other cities. "Wednesday's Child" features routinely include messages like, "This child has had a difficult past, but with loving parents, it is felt she will be able to overcome these problems."

Critics charge that such features knowingly mislead parents into claiming children they may not be equipped to cope with. They say potential parents should be aware that more questions must be answered before they agree to adopt:

- What is the truth about the child? Has the child been abused? Sexually abused? At what age? How severely? Can the crisis be overcome?
- Was the disclosure complete? Has she been neglected? When? What are the possible consequences? What will be required? Where is help available?

Although the caseworkers' intentions usually are good when they provide the "Wednesday's Child" story lines—finding homes for homeless children—their misrepresentations have heartbreaking consequences. Six sets of parents from Texas found that out the hard way. They all adopted children featured in "Wednesday's Child" segments, and all had severe psychological problems that required years of expensive therapy. None was aware of these problems when they agreed to adopt the child.

The couples made national news by filing a class-action suit against the Texas Department of Human Services in 1987, charging the agency with deceptive trade practices. They asked for help with therapy costs, for rules that required a complete disclosure of children's pasts before they are adopted and for better training programs for adoptive parents and more state-supported counseling for their children.

Neil Cogan, the assistant dean of the Southern Methodist University Law School and the attorney who filed their lawsuit, told *Texas Monthly*, "The parents say [the agency] glossed over or withheld information about their children. In effect, [the agency] placed children in the homes of these parents without telling them who the children were, and then, when these human time bombs exploded, [the agency] had no help to offer."[4]

Parents usually receive a written summary of the child's records, but the "Texas Six," as they became known, demanded more than this typically glossed-over version of the records. They asked for access to all files, excluding identification material such as the names and addresses of biological parents. Experts agree that full disclosure is the only way to avoid the sorts of problems these parents experienced.

The authors add that it is the caseworker's job to ferret out the information, even when it isn't easy to find. Not to do so can lead to disasters like the Chandlers'.

THE CHANDLERS

The Rev. Bob Chandler, senior minister for Highlands Christian Church in Dallas, and his wife, Cherry, are part of the lawsuit mentioned above. The daughter they adopted required residential treatment at a private clinic that specializes in attachment issues.

Like so many other couples, the Chandlers thought of adoption as the socially responsible way to build a family. With two birth sons, they decided to adopt a daughter. The girl who arrived in November, 1978, had been featured on "Wednesday's Child" as a perfectly normal three-year-old. They actually were delighted that Tina didn't shed a tear when they picked her up from the foster home. They later were horrified to learn that this was a sign of attachment disorder. Their new daughter was unable to form close relationships and had severe behavioral problems that surfaced slowly.

The first signs were vandalism, then constant "crazy" lies that made no sense and stealing things that ranged from her mother's jewelry to $150 in store merchandise. When Tina was ten, she set fire to her brothers' blue jeans. At eleven, she took out a butcher knife and hacked up living-room furniture. Then she threatened to kill her brothers.

"One psychiatrist told us she could kill us in the night and never shed a tear," says Cherry Chandler.[5]

A lawyer helped them obtain records from the Department of Human Services that revealed Tina had been severely sexually abused as an infant. The records included pictures of the child's badly bruised genitals that made Cherry want to "crawl off and die."

When the records were discovered, the Chandlers sent Tina to the Attachment Center in Evergreen, Colorado, for treatment. She underwent holding sessions to reduce the rage caused by the early abuse that was locked deep within her psyche. When Tina came home from the clinic, the Chandlers noticed her first authentic feelings of love.

She is, at the time of this writing, doing well at home, but will need ongoing therapy to keep her from slipping back into past rage. Fortunately, the state of Texas now pays for her counseling and that of any child under eighteen for whom the state acted as conservator or provided adoption assistance. That accounts for about 8,200 children who passed through the state's system between 1980 and 1990, an estimated 35 percent of whom were returned to the agency by adoptive parents unable to cope with their problems.

The Chandlers and Tina have been outspoken about her adoption and treatment, appearing on several national television shows. After an appearance on *Donahue* in 1989, more than six hundred people wrote to the Attachment Disorders Parents Network in Boulder, Colorado. The Chandlers blame the Department of Human Services for withholding information about Tina's past and for delaying her treatment. Like the other Texas parents, they say they don't know if they would have adopted Tina if they had known what they now know.

"These kids need more help than any one family can possibly provide," Bob Chandler says.[6]

MARK

Diane and M. L. Richards weren't as lucky as the Chandlers. They adopted seven-year-old Mark, then found out he had been diagnosed as mentally ill even before they took him. A psychologist later diagnosed him as a "borderline personality," a violent boy who was unable to form social relationships.

Only when Mark was admitted to a private mental hospital that cost nearly $15,000 a month were they able to get a copy of his adoption files. (By that time, however, the Richards' family insurance was exhausted.) The agency files showed that he had been mentally ill long before the adoption, and that his prognosis a year before he came into their home was "poor."

As a child, Mark had been starved by his mother and sexually molested. His father was responsible for Mark's missing left forefinger—he had bitten it off. Says Diane Richards, tears filling her eyes, "There's a part of Mark we love, and there's a part of him we loathe."

The Dynamics of "Stretching"

In June, 1984, Lynn and John Davis watched the Channel 8 news in Dallas. A young black child named Michael appeared on the screen, and the Davises said they instantly felt like reaching into the set and embracing the four-year-old. When they called the Department of Human Services, however, they were directed to a group of four troubled black siblings. They call it a classic case of "bait and switch." They say they "were stretched" to take on more children—and more problems—than they were ready for.

Also stretched, they say, was the truth. Caseworkers played down the severity of their children's abuse, which in fact had been quite brutal. They opened their home to the four children in July, 1985, and they immediately began to "act out." Lynn Davis spent most of her time trying to keep them from sexually abusing each other and other children. She eventually had to quit her job, and the couple's marriage was injured by the trauma. They are trying to keep the children together in spite of the hardships, but as Lynn describes it, "Our life is a living hell."

Texas psychologist Barbara Rila says these children never should have been placed together in one home. "Their internal cores have been shredded," she explains. "Parenting one of them would have been an incredible challenge; four are impossible."[7]

A federal district judge in Dallas who heard these parents' stories denied their requests; his ruling still is under appeal. However, the lawsuit did spur Texas legislators to clean up the methods used by caseworkers in adoption cases.

In 1989, Rev. Chandler worked with Texas Rep. Frank Collasco and Sen. Chet Brooks on a law that requires the state to provide post-adoption counseling and mandates that all information on a child be given to prospective parents. The law went into effect in March, 1990, earmarking $3.4 million for therapy that year and another $4.6 million in 1991. A Post-Adoption Services Advisory Committee also was set up to help eligible families tap into the services.

What the Laws Say

Until Texas took the lead in 1990, individual states had avoided the issue of wrongful adoptions. In 1986, the Ohio Supreme Court heard the *Burr v. Board of County Commissioners of Stark County* case (23 Ohio St. 3d 69 [11986]) and awarded $125,000 in damages to adoptive parents who got their son from a county agency twenty-two years earlier.

The Court found that the agency had committed fraud when it placed the child with the Burrs without telling them the truth about his background. The agency argued that it had immunity and the right to confidentiality, but the court ruled that those rights did not supersede the parents' right to know.

By that time, three states—Kansas, Illinois and New York—had laws requiring that adoptive parents be given genetic, medical and social histories of children. After the Texas Six lawsuit, Texas also added a law that requires disclosure of all records for all children placed by the state, excluding any that would identify biological parents. For a complete, state-by-state listing of laws, refer to the *Adoption Factbook*, published by the National Committee for Adoption.

Why People Try

Why do families take on these severely abused youngsters? There is no one answer, but court cases reveal that many do so with no idea what they're getting into. "Many have vague expectations based on a fantasy," says psychologist Barbara Rila. "They need the accurate information [on the child's background] to build onto their expectations."

It is possible to help the children who so desperately need that vital attachment and connection to a loving, consistent parent, Rila says, although each child will require an individualized approach. Older children need the chance to express the pain and rage caused by their abuse. Their parents will be called on to be patient, loving and caring, even when they can not take away their children's pain or reverse the damage caused by prenatal drug or alcohol abuse.

One adoptive father said he often reflects on his adopted child's needs, "especially when I'm sitting back, relaxing in the hot tub." He often asks himself, "Why did we do this? Would we do it again?" He isn't sure they would.

The authors do not want to destroy the hopes and dreams of would-be parents, and we certainly don't want to discourage anyone from adopting a special-needs child. Raising any child brings good times and bad times, and in that sense adopted children are no different. When rage subsides and these children overcome problems, adoptive parents can revel in the knowledge that they helped make that possible. Armed with full background information and helped with adequate support, these special parents can help Wednesday's Children lead successful, happy lives.

---

[1] Jan Jarboe, *Texas Monthly* (August 1988): p. 89.

[2] Ibid., p. 87.

[3] National Commission on Children, *Just the Facts: A Summary of Recent Information on America's Children and Their Families*, 1993, p. 154.

[4] Jan Jarboe, *Texas Monthly,* p. 146.

[5] Ibid., p. 148.

[6] Bob Chandler, *Attachments*, 1990.

[7] Barbara Rila, personal interview, May 1991.

CHAPTER SIX

ATTACHMENT ISSUES

Our personal involvement in the
fight against evil in the world
is one of the ways we grow.
M. Scott Peck, M.D.,
The Road Less Traveled

One of the most insidious problems adopted children can bring with them is an attachment disorder. Children who are abused, neglected and mistreated to the degree that they can no longer love or trust any adult become unattached children who, without supportive homes and strong therapy, may grow up to become tomorrow's sociopaths.

Levi's Story

The first time Dianna Lynn White laid eyes on Levi, the frightened three-and-a-half-year-old child was huddled in a corner. Other children were happily playing nearby, but he could not join in. At the time, Dianna was holding her infant daughter, Megan, and was five months pregnant with Alicia, but she realized Levi needed help.

Dianna knew his mother, "Christy." They were foster sisters as children, but all Dianna knew now was that Christy had been hopelessly addicted to cocaine for years. She didn't know that Levi bore the brunt of his mother's drug-induced sexual abuse until the Whites rescued him.

"I was naive," Dianna says, sitting in her living room. "We didn't know then the extent of the abuse and what it meant to Levi's life." Only after years of therapy did the terrible truth come out. During his first three years, Levi was burned with cigarettes, forced to perform oral sex, abandoned for long periods of time and punished by having small toys stuffed up his rectum.

Before they found out the extent of his abuse and torture, the Whites knew something was very wrong with Levi. He could not love, he threw hour-long fits of rage and he was capable of hurting the people who loved him. Only when he severely burned Megan's hand and dislocated Alicia's shoulder did they realize he needed more help than they could give him.

At eight, Levi is now living in a therapeutic foster home where experts are trying to bring him to terms with his painful past. He may never come home from the residential treatment center. His condition: attachment disordered.

The second most critical need during infancy is developing an attachment to a significant adult. (The first is having physical needs met.) The bond that develops between a child and his primary care giver is the basis for all future relationships and psychological development. The primary care giver can be a birth parent, foster parent or adoptive parent. It doesn't matter as long as the child has one consistent care giver during the first two years of life.

During that "attachment cycle," the infant experiences a need (either pain, hunger or discomfort), expresses that need and elicits a response (touch, eye contact, motion, food) that gratifies the need. It is the repetition of this gratification, thousands of times without interruption during the first two years, that forms a strong trust bond between the child and the care giver.

Attachment is an affectionate bond between two individuals that endures through time and space and joins them emotionally. It also affects children's ability to form close relationships throughout their lives, and helps them:

- Attain full intellectual potential;
- Sort out perceptions;
- Think logically;
- Develop a conscience;
- Become self-reliant;
- Cope with stress and frustration;
- Handle fear and worry; and
- Reduce jealousy.[1]

THE ATTACHMENT CYCLE

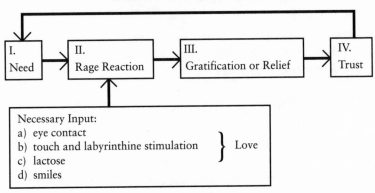

The bond of trust and attachment later helps the child accept limits and controls as they are imposed by parents. An interruption of the cycle can occur when there is: separation from, or change of, primary care giver; abuse or neglect; chronic and unrelieved pain; or gratification without touch, motion or eye contact. The interruption is called a "bonding break."

Children who have experienced interruptions of the attachment cycle during the first two years of life will later exhibit some of the following symptoms of attachment-disordered children. They will:

- Seem superficially engaging and "charming";
- Lack eye contact;
- Be indiscriminately affectionate with strangers;

- Not be affectionate or cuddly with care givers;
- Be destructive to self, others and material things—sometimes considered accident-prone;
- Be cruel to animals;
- Lie about the obvious/"crazy lying";
- Have no impulse controls (frequently act hyperactive);
- Have learning lags;
- Seem not to understand cause and effect;
- Lack a conscience;
- Have abnormal eating patterns;
- Relate poorly with peers;
- Be preoccupied with fire;
- Ask persistent nonsense questions and chatter incessantly;
- Be inappropriately demanding and clingy; and
- Have abnormal speech patterns.[2]

Some children arrive in the system with attachment disorders; others, ironically, get them from the system set up to help them. The latter's attachment disorders occur as they are bounced from one foster home to another, constantly experiencing "breaks."

Specialist Selma Fraiberg describes the process this way: "When, for any reason, a child has spent the whole or a large part of his infancy in an environment that could not provide him with human partners or the conditions for sustained human attachments, the later development of the child demonstrates measurable effects."[3]

Fraiberg says unattached children have three specific problem areas:

1. They form relationships only on the basis of need, with little regard for one care giver over another. Their capacity to attach to any one person is impaired.
2. Their development is retarded and does not improve over time. Conceptual thinking remains low, even when favorable environments are provided for the children in the second and third years of life. Language itself, which was grossly retarded in all the infant studies, improves under

more favorable environmental conditions but is never fully regained.

3. Disorders of impulse control, particularly in the area of aggression, were reported in all follow-up studies of these children.[4]

Experts speculate that even children adopted as infants can develop attachment problems because, as babies, they miss the voice and rhythm of the mother they bonded with *in utero*. However, these bonding problems are much easier to address in newborns. With proper intervention, including holding exercises, adoptive parents can teach their babies to attach emotionally to them.[5] The key, experts say, is having one consistent nurturing care giver available to the child during the formative first years, something the current child welfare system isn't always able to provide.

The Majority

In the adoption arena, there is a saying that it is "never wise to turn five." Because most prospective parents are looking for a healthy infant, children over five are hard to place. They are also the children who most often have attachment disorders, either because of abuse, neglect or length of stay in the child welfare system.

National Adoption Center figures show that 52 percent of all children available for adoption have some kind of emotional problem, and another study of children eligible for Medi-Cal in California found that those in foster care were hospitalized five times more often for mental health problems than other children.

Many of these children can be helped with adequate therapy, but it is in short supply. The U.S. Department of Housing and Human Services stated in 1990 that only about one in five children who need help get it. Early intervention and treatment are even harder to find. One study of black children in foster care found 41 percent of those ages six to twelve, and 80 percent of those under five, had not had mental health evaluations.[6]

Those children who do get treatment often end up in expensive, residential treatment centers, usually because it is the only kind of treatment covered by insurance. The facts are:

- Residential treatment of children has risen dramatically over the past several decades.
- Admission rates of youth in private psychiatric hospitals increased by 1,327 percent from 1971 to 1985.
- Thirty-seven states reported that 4,000 children were placed in out-of-state mental health facilities at a cost of $215 million. An additional 22,472 children were being treated in state hospitals.
- Fifty percent of youth in residential treatment receive care inappropriate for their situation.[7]

Members of the House Select Committee on Children, Youth and Families met in April, 1991, to study mental health concerns and acknowledged that the lack of treatment for youth causes a tremendous amount of suffering and imposes a costly burden on society. Costs for what mental health services are provided to children have risen to more than $3 billion a year. The cost of problems not being treated is even higher.

Angie Trenberth

Her name is Angie, as in "angel," but the similarity stops there. This curly-headed cutie was an angel from Hell.

When Gail and Kevin Trenberth first laid eyes on baby Angie, she was a battered eight-month-old infant with wispy blond hair. She crawled into their hearts, despite warnings that she had suffered severe abuse, including sexual abuse. The Trenberths were called on the spur of the moment by Illinois Social Services to see if they could provide temporary foster care for Angie and her sister, whose baby-sitter had called police to report their abuse.

At the time, the Trenberths were preparing to take their four-year-old birth daughter, Annika, to New Zealand, but they agreed to take the girls for three weeks. The girls stayed with another family while the Trenberths were out of the country, and three months after the family returned to Illinois, they were reunited with Angie. Her older sister stayed with another foster family.

"We foster-parented her for two years and had a chance to see she had problems," Gail says, "but we thought we could help her. We never dreamed how bad it would get, how badly scarred she was." Angie was so scarred that, as she grew, she:

- Was unable to get emotionally close to anyone;
- Acted out and was very demonstrative sexually;
- At ages four and five, turned the family into hermits because they could not take her out in public or invite friends to their home;
- Went up to guests and grabbed their private parts, tried to masturbate on their legs and put her hand down women's blouses.

"She was totally out of control," Gail says. "We didn't know then what we do now—that Angie was an unattached child. We didn't know how to get her the right treatment, and we felt helpless."

Like many adoptive parents of very troubled children, the Trenberths went ahead with the adoption in spite of the problems. "We felt that if we loved her enough and gave her a stable environment she would get well," Gail says.

Love was not enough. As Angie grew older, her bizarre behavior escalated. She was expelled from kindergarten after only three days and, faced with the choice of relinquishing Angie or placing her in an expensive residential treatment center, they chose the latter. After a year there, Angie was worse, not better, but the couple loved her and did not give up on her, even though their love was soon to meet its greatest test.

On a field trip one day, Angie bragged to other children that her adoptive father had sexually abused her. In what Gail calls a "totally unbelievable" twist of fate, the couple was brought before authorities and grilled. Although authorities eventually declared the couple innocent, they were devastated by the accusations. Gail was so hysterical that her doctor prescribed tranquilizers and nearly hospitalized her for a nervous breakdown.

"To this day, I suffer from medical problems caused by the stress of that time," Gail says with a sigh. For months, she could not sleep through the night. "I would get up and wander around the house, baking bread, washing floors."

Finally, the family found help. A psychologist referred them to the Attachment Center at Evergreen, Colorado. "For the first time I had hope that she might be able to be helped," Gail says. As Angie turned seven, she was placed in a therapeutic boarding program she would attend for two years. A "healing vacation" put distance between Angie and her adoptive mother, and Gail finally got some sleep.

"We didn't know what to expect, but they included us in the therapy sessions, and [we found that] Angie was a changed child," Gail says. "We couldn't believe it. Friends who knew her before have said, 'It is Angie's body, but there is another child in there.' We were ecstatic, but scared. I wasn't sure I could ever trust her."

Angie, now in her preteens, is a joy, her mother says. "She is well. She is cured. Oh, she still has a few small problems, but what child doesn't?" As for the trust, there are moments when Gail still hesitates. Most of the time, however, her little angel comes through for her.

"The other day we were chatting while I cooked dinner," Gail recounts. "She said, 'Mom, do you know what I want to be when I grow up? I want to be just like you.'"

Gail stammers, tears in her eyes, then says, "You know, no unattached child could ever say that! They *never* want to be like their mothers. I didn't know what to say, because I was all choked up."[8]

Angie Trenberth is one of the lucky ones. She found a family that could bond with her and work through the hard times.

Matching Pit Bulls with Collies

Psychologists and psychiatrists are beginning to realize the crisis attachment disorders cause for older adoptees. The first problem is correctly identifying children with attachment issues and matching them with parents equipped to cope with them. Dr. Foster Cline of Evergreen, Colorado, compares these children to "pit bulls" and normal, sane parents to "collies." "Collie" parents have certain expectations about their children, such as:

- Having a gentle, panting friendliness;
- Having a good understanding of cause and effect;

- Having a deep-down, heartfelt desire to be good;
- Being able to learn basic "German shepherd" commands, such as "come," "sit," "do" and "stay."

"When you have pit-bull [attachment-disordered] kids," Cline explains, "they have problems learning the basic commands. They may not want to learn, or they might get distracted learning. On the way to the sink to do the dishes, they might think of playing a video game. So they don't learn the basic 'German shepherd' commands their parents expect them to learn. They are capable of learning, but only if there isn't another kid there to chew on. Parents have to be constantly worried about the pit-bull kid killing all the others in the litter."[9]

A very disturbed child is unlikable, Cline cautions. "The disturbance makes it hard to like the kid, even though you love him and want to love him to pieces." And in too many cases, he adds, good foster or adoptive parents get blamed for the actions of the kids they get. "These kids know how to play the victim role," he says. "It's always, 'Poor me.' They really may be victims, but that is no excuse for their behavior."

What Problems Appear

Adopted children who are older than twelve have emotional problems that are significantly more intense and more frequent than comparable children who live with their birth families, according to a study done in 1991 by University of Northern Colorado researchers.

J. Lynn Rhodes and Ellis P. Copeland surveyed 388 adopted children placed by one Christian adoption group over the past twenty years, and compared them to a sample group of 290 birth children. They found the adopted group to be far more likely to exhibit deviant behaviors, including the symptoms of attachment disorders that stem from multiple bonding breaks in infancy. No one knows how many breaks must occur before a child begins to have attachment difficulties.

The researchers called the high percentage of deviance among adopted children "revealing to the point of being shocking," but found that many behaviors didn't show up until adolescence. Although the "roots of the [deviant] behavior may lie in early life experiences," the researchers wrote, "the fruit is not produced until adolescence."

The researchers compared the incidence of the following behaviors in both groups:

BEHAVIORS IN BIRTH AND ADOPTED CHILDREN

Behaviors	Birth	Adopted
▪ inability to give or receive affection	3.2	21.3
▪ phoniness	1.9	15.1
▪ self-control problems	3.9	26.3
▪ lack of long-term friends	4.5	21.9
▪ lying	3.9	25.7
▪ rejection of authority	1.3	30.0
▪ refusal to follow parental guidelines	3.2	25.8 [10]

The problems of unattached children can not be cured by holding, hugs and kisses, the kind of therapy most average parents are qualified to give. Many need intensive long-term therapy. In the past this therapy has been called "Rage Reduction Therapy"; it has evolved into a therapy known as "Reactive Attachment Disorder Therapy," or simply "Attachment Therapy." The outstanding characteristic of this intensive therapy is that the therapist becomes a "good boss" of the severely unattached child.

For example, the therapist uses various confrontational techniques in a loving, safe way to bring to the surface the hate the child has hidden deep inside but can not express. The reasons for that hate—abandonment as an infant, neglect, abuse or other physical pain—will also be brought to the surface. Out of this rage and pain come the child's lack of attachment and aloneness. These issues are addressed and the confusion of love versus hate (especially concerning the patient's birth mother) is confronted. The intent is to give the child a controlled, loving situation in which the unattached, untrusting child can explode into a more primordial rage and hate. Emotions run high. In this process feelings are brought to the surface under controlled conditions so the patient can deal with them once and for all without hurting himself or anyone else.

An important part of the therapy is the resolution toward the end of the session, after the "break through." The child is led through the reattachment process with a loving parent or care giver (usually the adopted parent). The therapist and parent know the reattachment process has started when the child has given up controlling mannerisms and resistance and given way to cooperation and comfortable give-and-take talk.[11]

Dr. Foster Cline has diagrammed the process, as follows:

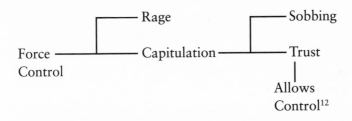

If therapy is to work, it is imperative that adoptive parents "know every single detail, every traumatic occurrence and the birth parents' history," says psychologist Barbara Rila of Texas.[13] "It also is necessary to get a professional assessment of the child from a trained therapist. Traumatic incidents have a direct and concrete result in subsequent traumas and the child's emotional behavior," says this expert on special-needs adoption and a founder of ATTACh, a national support group for people doing attachment therapies.

"A second major reason to know the past," she says, "is that children base later relationships on the earlier model of the original family." The horrifying truth is that many unattached, sexually abused children often become perpetrators themselves. With the help of a qualified therapist, the child can be taught healthier ways to cope with the abuse.

Repairing the Damage

It is society's responsibility to shift the emphasis away from adoption as a means of providing children to parents, and replace it with the goal of providing stable, caring supportive parents for needy children. Such parents are rare, and more must be recruited, but if they are to be successful, they will need more than love to get them through the trying times. They will need all the support and help the system can muster. Special-needs children with attachment disorders require special full-time parents who do not quickly become exhausted, but their efforts can pay off. Good parenting and a positive environment can help children overcome bad beginnings. The key seems to be consistency.

There is much to be learned from the work of the National Association for Perinatal Addiction, Research and Education (NAPARE), a Chicago group that is using early intervention to help damaged babies and their birth mothers. It has come up with a specific list of recommendations for parents taking care of drug-exposed babies. The Attachment Center at Evergreen also has a brochure on parenting challenged and unattached children (see Appendix III).

It is imperative that everyone working with a challenged child knows as much as possible about her background and the genetic factors that may be influencing behavior. Once the challenges have been diagnosed, it is also imperative that parents are trained to recognize and deal with them. Special-needs children must be placed in a predictable, positive environment with parents who are committed for the long term to healing them. The quality of the environment, not quality time, is the solution.

We do not need blame. We must get past the blame to the solutions, which include taking a hard look at our society and how it deals with the issues that cause the problems:

- *Irresponsible birth parents.* These parents and teens are victims themselves. A society that preaches "Just Say No" simply isn't in tune with the challenge. We must give addicted birth mothers help so they can defeat their need to escape reality. We must also do special screening tests on all babies born to mothers suspected of abusing drugs. Equally important is training adopting parents, foster parents, caseworkers and medical personnel to recognize drug abuse symptoms and know how to treat them.
- *Abusive parents.* Often they carry on the cycle they have known as children. Recent reports show child abuse in America is growing exponentially. It is imperative we support the efforts of those fighting child abuse in America, and organizations like the

Kempe National Center, a center for research on the prevention of child abuse. But we must not overreact and unnecessarily pull children from their birth homes. There are excellent models for family preservation that work, including those developed by the Edna McConnell Clark Foundation in Washington, D.C. When family preservation is impossible, out-of-home placement may be the best choice for children, but the goal must always be to find them a permanent placement, and quickly.

- *Children placed randomly and repeatedly.* A system that shuffles children from place to place with little regard for the outcome is abusive. The foster care system must begin to plan permanent homes for children from the moment they arrive. Parents—adoptive and foster—must be given the tools they need to manage difficult children. The Adoption Assistance and Child Welfare Act of 1980 provides federal assistance for services that enable children to remain with birth families and mandates that children who must be removed are assured "eventual returns to safe birth homes, or timely placement with adoptive families to establish permanent, loving and culturally sensitive homes."[14] We must demand that it be followed.

- *A lack of prenatal care.* All women, no matter how poor, should have access to public health services, prenatal care and drug abuse treatment. Prevention programs for drug abusers, such as counseling, birth control and prenatal care, go a long way in helping prevent some of these situations.[15] Drug-abusing women should be given birth control options, such as NORPLANT, to protect them from pregnancy during their withdrawal from drugs, and those already pregnant should be given intensive prenatal care and intervention. Model programs have achieved success, but the key is meeting the needs of their clients. These successful programs offer Saturday appointments, transportation, child care and increased cultural sensitivity.

- *Ignorant judicial system and therapeutic community.* Judges often make wrong decisions for children because they don't have all the facts. They should be taught to determine the nature of present attachments and to use personality- and temperament-matching instruments before passing judgment on a child's future. Another undereducated group is the therapeutic community, many of whom do not recognize the illnesses of damaged children. Few therapists are trained to provide the type of therapy necessary to enable the attachment-disordered child to develop a strong, positive bond with his or her new parents. We believe more trained professionals will be necessary in the future.

- *A country that doesn't value families.* What do we do about a system that does not value children? The solution will require a commitment from all levels of our society: churches, schools, the therapeutic community, lawmakers, business and the general public. Society will have to take on these damaged offspring. We don't need unfair stereotyping of these children. We do need parents who:

1. Can be loving, responsive, able to provide consistent discipline and deal with the child's fear, uncertainty and rejecting behavior;
2. Can understand and relate to the types of problems their child will likely bring to their home;
3. Are prepared for these problems through pre- and postadoption counseling, and receive all the support the system can give them, including respite care and financial help;
4. Are matched in temperament to the youngster before the foster care or adoption takes place;
5. Have the resources to make at least one attachment figure available to the challenged child at all times, either the mother, the father or another individual such as a grandparent or nanny who will be available for the long haul. The national Family Leave Law, passed in 1993, should make this task easier.

- *Clear attachment disorders.* Parents with difficult children may have to use rather strict parenting methods. They may have to handle the children in a hard way (such as "tough love") to make them responsible. Private educational systems, such as

Accelerated Schools in Denver or military-type boarding schools, may offer some help. These parents must have support in their quest to help their children.

It is time for the judicial system, psychologists, psychiatrists, therapists, teachers and foster/adoptive parents to forge a coalition to guarantee early intervention for these babies and a lifelong commitment to the nation's hurting children.

Conclusions

The neediest of the children caught in the system are those who dared to turn five in the foster care/adoption system or who were abused *in utero* or after birth. Most suffer from attachment disorders. As their numbers grow—an estimated four million drug-exposed children are on their way—the systems set up to help them are floundering. The problems are compounded by a legal system that isn't well educated about their special needs, and a mental health system that is often unprepared to provide the necessary therapy.

FOR SUCCESSFUL PLACEMENTS

It is possible to use the following techniques to place children successfully.

1. Matching, to take the guesswork aspect out of placement.
2. Preadoption training to prepare adoptive families for the challenges ahead.
3. Postplacement follow-up and education to make sure the child and family are assimilating in a healthy fashion, using family preservation techniques.
4. Some adoption subsidies to help with problems encountered when adoptive families can not afford the expense of caring for their children who have physical or mental problems.

Properly prepared foster and adoptive parents can make a differ-ence. We know that families—working in unison with professionals—can come to understand these children. Our greatest need is for more "special" families to take on these "special-needs" children. They are innocent victims of birth parents who are unable to fulfill their re-sponsibilities. Unless better ways can be found to save them, they also will become "throw-away children," victims of a society unable to provide for its own.

---

[1] Vera Fahlberg, M.D., *Attachment and Separation*, 1979, p. 5.

[2] Foster Cline, M.D.,"Understanding and Treating the Severely Disturbed Child," *What Shall We Do with This Child*, 1979, p. 28.

[3] Selma Fraiberg, *Every Child's Birthright: In Defense of Mothering* (Basic Books, 1977): pp. 51–54.

[4] Ibid.

[5] Rep. George Miller, U.S. House Select Committee on Children, Youth and Fami-lies, Fall 1989.

[6] U.S. House Select Committee on Children, Youth and Families, *Adolescent Health Report*, Office of Technology Assessment, April 1991.

[7] Ibid.

[8] Gail Trenberth, personal interview, Boulder, Colorado, June 1991.

[9] Foster Cline, M.D., personal interview, Evergreen, Colorado, January 1991.

[10] J. Lynn Rhodes and Ellis P. Copeland, *Dysfunctional Behavior in Adopted Chil-dren: Behavior Differences between Adopted and Birth Children*, University of North-ern Colorado, November 1991.

[11] Ken Magid and Carole McKelvey, *High Risk: Children without a Conscience*, (NewYork: Bantam, 1988): pp. 211–13.

[12] Foster Cline, M.D., *What Shall We Do with This Child?*, p. 162.

[13] Barbara Rila, M.D., personal interview, Atlanta, Georgia, July 1991.

[14] *User's Guide to Public Law 96-272: A Summarization and Codification of Admin-istrative Regulations* is now available from the North American Council on Adoptable Children for $50 plus postage and handling. Write NACAC, 1821 University Ave., Suite N-498, St. Paul, MN 55104.

[15] California Gov. Pete Wilson, *Ventura County Star-Free Press,* July 19, 1991, p. C-4.

CHAPTER SEVEN

CHALLENGED CHILDREN

*"Parentage is a very important profession; but no test of fitness
for it is ever imposed in the interest of the children."*
George Bernard Shaw,
Everybody's Political What's What

As if it's not enough that more children are entering foster care and staying there longer, caseworkers have another challenge facing them by the year 1995. An estimated four million babies damaged by their mother's drug abuse, another forty thousand babies exposed *in utero* to alcohol abuse and twenty thousand exposed to HIV will be cared for by the child welfare system. Their problems are unique and very difficult to cope with. Take Stephanie Bolding, for example.

Stephanie Bolding

Stephanie's mother was on an intense LSD trip when her labor started six weeks early. Her doctors had to sedate the woman so they could deliver her tiny 4-pound, 12-ounce daughter. Fos/Adopt mother Kimm Bolding was there to soothe the trembling baby, but it was harder than she had anticipated.

Stephanie, the white, black and possibly Korean daughter of a prostitute, was exposed to more than LSD while still a fetus. Her mother also had used marijuana, crack cocaine and alcohol while pregnant, but she neglected to talk about her drug abuse when she asked Kimm and Gregory Bolding to raise her unborn child.

"Her mother lied to us," says Bolding. "She told us she wasn't using. We said we'd take the baby if it was a healthy girl with no drugs involved. We got one out of three."[1]

The first few weeks of her life, Stephanie slept only twenty minutes at a time. The Boldings took turns caring for her so each could get some sleep. And there were times when they "lost" Stephanie for a few minutes, Kimm says. Several times she stopped her car in the middle of the road, ignoring traffic while she resuscitated the child.

Like most drug-exposed babies, Stephanie responded to affection with screams and irritability. The slightest touch hurt her, causing her to withdraw from her adoptive mother's touch. "We cried along with her," Kimm says through tears. "I've cried every day since Stephanie was born [because] ... I know the pain this little one is going through, and it's so hard to face."

Because of her mother's substance abuse during pregnancy, Stephanie suffered from "sleep apnea" (breathing problems that interrupt her sleep and threaten to kill her) and was on constant oxygen and a breathing monitor. She was at high risk for sudden infant death syndrome (SIDS); she had tremors and seizures; and her "reflux" (gagging mechanism) was so strong that she constantly threw up after eating.

Like many parents who have taken on these challenged infants, the Boldings had trouble finding doctors who understood Stephanie's problems. They eventually turned to Dr. Ira Chasnoff of NAPARE (the National Association for Perinatal Addiction Research and Education) for a referral—Dr. Sharon Langendorfer of Denver General Hospital, the only neonatologist in the Rocky Mountain region at the time who was an expert on drug babies.

By thirteen weeks old, Kimm says, Stephanie had come through the roughest times. "Her breathing problems seemed to be getting better, she was sleeping three to four hours at a time, and her apnea monitor was going off less." Early tests found that Stephanie also suffers from optic nerve damage, shaking of her eyes caused by fetal alcohol syndrome, neurological problems associated with dark spots found on the white matter of her brain, an atrophy of the brain that caused the distance between her skull and brain to be enlarged and an immaturity of the brain cortex.

"The good news is that she's HIV-negative," says Kimm, "and they found no abnormalities in her renal and genital organs, where drug babies often have problems."

The bad news? Her birth mother is pregnant again.

The Boldings are already raising Stephanie's half brother, a four-year-old with fetal alcohol syndrome. "I'm fairly close with Stephanie's mom, and she finally told me about her drug use," Kimm says. "She said that when she took the LSD, she could feel Stephanie 'scratching and kicking inside,' like she knew it was going to kill her if she didn't ... come out early."

Sighing, Kimm says, "I guess that is just something [the woman] will have to live with herself."

Thousands of Drug Babies

In recent years, expectant mothers have exposed their babies to a plethora of drugs, ranging from alcohol to opiates and barbiturates to cocaine. When crack cocaine came on the scene in the mid-1980s, the inexpensive, smokeable and extremely addictive substance became the drug of choice for women of childbearing age. By 1986, an estimated 40 percent of all people between twenty and thirty years old had tried the drug, and many of their children paid the price.[2]

Unlike certain drugs and chemicals that can cause malformation of the fetus only if taken during the first three months of pregnancy, crack cocaine can cause deformities at any stage. It interferes with the blood flow to the already perfectly formed organs, causing them to become deformed.

Unfortunately, this is particularly true of the brain. Studies at hospitals have shown the terrible long-term damage crack cocaine can do to children. In one study of seventy-four full-term cocaine- and methamphetamine-exposed infants, researchers found that 35.1 percent had cranial abnormalities (compared to 5.3 percent of non-drug-exposed babies). The damage to the frontal lobes and basal ganglia became evident after the first year, when more complex visual motor and social tasks were needed. In addition, delayed athetoid cerebral palsy may occur.[3]

At birth, children exposed to crack cocaine exhibit a variety of symptoms that make them difficult to care for. They have problems keeping down their food because of reflux. They are also prone to spasms, trembling and rigid muscles. Many are born premature and medically fragile, with birth defects that cause physical and mental handicaps. They resist cuddling by arching their backs, a sign of possibly lasting nervous system damage that can lead to emotional disorders. They can also go from short-term restless sleep to screaming alertness, with nothing in between.

Babies exposed prenatally to cocaine have exhibited "hollowness, lethargy, unresponsiveness and sudden unpredictable outbursts of violence and aggression, characteristics that set them apart from other poor or homeless children," says Dr. Judy Howard of Los Angeles.[4]

The most severely challenged crack cocaine babies have a stiffening of their hands, a trancelike gaze and difficulty sucking and eating. At nine months, they display fine motor coordination problems. At twenty-four months, they have speech articulation problems.

Although researchers won't have hard data for several decades about the effects of drug exposure on children, some preliminary studies have found problems with concentration and learning. In one research group, 25 percent of drug-exposed children had developmental delays, 40 percent had neurologic abnormalities that might affect their ability to socialize and function within a school environment and all had problems with language, adaptive behavior, fine motor and cognitive skills.[5]

These are children with serious problems, Judith Schaffer told the North American Council on Adoptable Children's 16th annual conference in 1991, not "children for parents whose lifestyles are better suited to 'quality' versus 'quantity time' parenting."[6]

Babies who are born with more than one drug in their system are unable to regulate themselves. This means, for example, that they can not go from sleeping to being fully awake without screaming and tremors. One study found this to be the only abnormal characteristic from newborn to age five, but Dr. Howard disagrees. Like other experts, she has predicted that new psychological problems will arise with age and wonders what these drug-exposed infants will be like when they are eighteen years old.

Many drug-exposed children don't survive that long, succumbing during their first year to SIDS. Such was the fate of one-month-old Linda. Her Aunt Maria tells the story two days after Linda's death:

> I just wasn't prepared to see a baby die. My little girl was holding her just an hour before. She had some problems, but none of us thought they were real problems. I went to pick her up and realized she wasn't breathing. It was awful. They tried to revive her, but she was already dead.

"Maria" begins to cry as she explains that her sister, the baby's mother, used cocaine and alcohol throughout her pregnancy. "The baby died at just one month old, and I know it was the cocaine," she sobs.[7]

This crisis of *in utero* drug abuse captured the nation's attention in 1989, when the House Select Committee on Children, Youth and Families studied the extent of the problem. About eighteen major municipal hospitals were asked how many pregnant patients used drugs, and many reported an increase in birth mothers addicted to cocaine, heroin, PCP, marijuana and other drugs.[8] They also reported an increase in babies born drug-exposed, up from 12 percent in 1985 to more than 15 percent by 1988. One hospital in Denver, Colorado, for example, reported 32 drug-exposed newborns in 1985 and 115 in 1988.

Additional research shows that between 10 and 20 percent of all pregnant women admit to using cocaine at some time during their pregnancy. And even when a mother claims to be drug-free, urine screens often indicate otherwise. In one study, 26 percent of the pregnant women who tested positive for cocaine denied having used it.[9]

Other studies found that pregnant women who abuse crack cocaine are prone to death during labor and delivery, are more likely to have sexually transmitted diseases and are at higher risk of HIV infection. No one knows exactly how many drug-exposed babies are born each year, but the General Accounting Office estimates there are at least 400,000[10]. Another study found that, in 1991, New York City spent $500 million on hospital care for thousands of drug-exposed babies.[11]

California Governor Pete Wilson lashed out at these "irresponsible parents" in 1991, vowing the state would have "zero tolerance" for those saddling the public with drug-exposed children. Wilson said society should not have to do the job of parents, but should instead provide prevention programs for drug abusers, including such programs as birth control, counseling and prenatal care.[12]

The California governor blamed dysfunctional families for driving teenagers to drugs and into each other's arms to find solace. The exposed babies they bear become society's burdens. In New York City, for example, most of the infants coming into foster care are born to women abusing cocaine or crack. This abuse is escalating as street prices drop and as teenagers use the drug at much younger ages than ever before.

Although the right kind of prenatal care could lessen the severity of drug exposure problems, agencies make little effort to provide it to substance abusers. One study found that pregnant women who abuse drugs or alcohol are four times less likely than the average woman to get prenatal care, and as many as 70 percent of them get no prenatal care at all. That compares to 15 percent of the general population.

Significant roadblocks exist between these women and either drug treatment or prenatal care:

- Many are unaware of the effects of drug use on their babies;
- Others who are aware of the consequences would like to stop using drugs but either don't have access to drug treatment facilities or are afraid they will be jailed or their children will be taken away from them;
- Some can't afford even the most basic health care services, even though the U.S. Office of Technology Assessment estimates that prenatal care can save money. Studies show that $500 worth of prenatal care can prevent between $14,000 and $30,000 in short- and long-term health costs for each low-birth-weight baby.[13]

The Value of Intervention

It is easy to become discouraged about the future of these drug-exposed children if you believe all the experts' predictions, but not everyone believes these children are doomed. With postnatal intervention, Dr. Chasnoff and the staff at NAPARE think the prognosis "is encouraging" and hope their research is proving that drug-exposed children can be salvaged if they get the right kind of intensive therapy. They are finding that the best place for these children is in a permanent home.

The group followed three hundred babies cocaine-exposed at birth and enrolled them with their mothers in an intensive postnatal intervention. Preliminary tests of ninety children at age three revealed that:

- 90 percent showed normal intelligence;
- 70 percent had no behavioral problems; and
- 60 percent did not need speech therapy.[14]

Fos/Adopt mother Debbe Magnusen of Costa Mesa, California, agrees with this assessment. Over the years, she and her husband, David, have had twenty-one foster children, and now they are raising four drug-exposed children who range in age from six months to five years. All appear to be normal, Debbe says.[15]

This couple didn't start out with the idea of providing a permanent home for drug-exposed babies. Debbe shrugs, "There's an old saying—one thing leads to another, and in our case, that led to adoption."

SYMPTOMS OF A CRACK BABY

- Stiffening of the hands
- Trancelike glaze in the eyes
- Trouble sucking and eating
- Fine motor coordination problems
- Speech articulation problems

The Children

Bee Jay was the first drug baby to arrive at the Magnusens' five years ago. They got a call from social services one night asking if they could take a child who was exposed in the womb to schizophrenic behavior and cocaine. When he arrived, Debbe says, he was a mess.

"We really had to work with that kid to get him to bond with us," she says. "Then, at about three months old, he finally began cooing and smiling. I made a mistake and let another person feed him [and] ... he just went away. I had to put my hands on both sides of his little face and make him look at us. Finally, a bunch of us laid him on the bed and got our faces close and just stared at him. He went crazy, squirming all around trying not to look at us [a common reaction of drug babies called 'gaze aversion']. But, finally, he got contact again."

The episode made her realize she had to be extra sensitive with Bee Jay—devote even more time and pay even more attention to him than before. This tiny child taught them how to parent drug-exposed babies.

"His birth mother would come to see him, and he would throw up when he saw her," Debbe says. "He *knew* who she was [and what she had done to him], even though she had given him up at five days old!"

"That first year was horrible," she remembers, but then came "the others":

- Four-year-old Beth was born to a cocaine- and alcohol-addicted mother;
- Three-year-old Emily was born to a cocaine/heroine/methadone mother and was on an apnea monitor her first two years;
- Six-month-old Tyler was born in a toilet by a mother so high on amphetamines and cocaine she didn't realize she was in labor.

Debbe believes all her children will grow up to lead normal lives, but first they face major challenges. The first supreme hurdle comes between their second and fifth months of life when they go through drug withdrawal. "Imagine what they go through," Debbe says. "These chemicals are trapped in their livers until birth, when they are excreted." She has seen babies become "suicidal" after the first few months because they aren't getting any more of the drug.

"It's gone, and they go into a depressed state," Debbe explains. "They become 'failure-to-thrive' babies. They don't know what happened. They know they felt great and now this!"

None of the Magnusens' adopted children have entered school yet, and when they do, more problems may arise. No one really knows how drug exposure affects children's ability to learn, but the first studies aren't promising. The first wave of crack babies entered school in 1991, and early reports are that some of the drug's effects don't show themselves until children confront the more complex tasks they encounter in the classroom.

Early estimates are that the nation's schools soon will be deluged with a "huge cadre of cocaine-exposed children who are, in fact, severely disabled but whose handicaps have until now not been picked up."[16] A preliminary study of forty-six children exposed to drugs as fetuses found that all had intelligence scores in the low-normal range at two years old and all had ongoing nervous system problems.[17]

Researchers suspect that, by school age, drug-exposed children will show signs of hyperactivity, retardation, learning impairments and speech and motor delays. Magnusen and other parents of drug-exposed children disagree, saying that early intervention and knowledgeable parents can prevent such problems, and speakers at a NAPARE convention urged participants not to label the children until more research can be done.[18] Even so, it is clear that the costs of these children to the system don't stop at the hospital doors or in their foster care or adoptive homes.

Fetal Alcohol Syndrome

Fetal alcohol syndrome (FAS) is the leading cause of mental retardation in the United States and one of three leading causes of birth defects. No one knows how many children have it, but experts agree that forty thousand children in America would be spared each year if prenatal exposure to alcohol could be prevented.[19]

Alcohol use has serious implications on the development of a child, and can lead to such things as lower IQ levels, hyperactivity and impaired development of the central nervous system.[20] Children who suffer from the condition often have facial deformities described as "pixie"-like, with wide-set eyes, a flat nose, lack of a rose-bud mouth and an unusual increase in the amount of fine hair on the forehead and upper face at birth.

A less severe problem, called fetal alcohol effect (FAE), can occur when a birth mother drinks more moderately during the first three months of gestation, when her child's brain is developing. This condition is harder to detect but just as serious in that it can mentally challenge a child for life. Children who have it often have difficulty concentrating, are clumsy and have learning disabilities, but they do not have distorted facial characteristics.

Because Native American and Eskimo populations have particularly high alcoholism rates, their children are being devastated by the effects of FAS and FAE. Native American babies, for example, are thirty times more likely to have one of the two conditions than Anglo babies.[21]

Experts believe these disadvantaged children, like those exposed to drugs *in utero*, may benefit most from being placed with well-prepared adoptive parents. As Judith Schaffer told participants in the North American Council on Adoptable Children's 1991 conference, "A permanent commitment by well-prepared adoptive parents can be the best intervention the child receives."[22]

HIV and AIDS

Drugs and alcohol are not the only two damaging things children can be exposed to *in utero*. Mothers who are infected with HIV, the virus thought to cause AIDS, also can pass it along to their children. Not all children born to HIV-positive mothers get the deadly virus, but those who do face a short and challenged life. Many are abandoned by mothers who themselves are under a death sentence, and even those lucky enough to find temporary foster homes face uncertainty.

MICKEY

Mickey spent the first ten months of his life in a New York City hospital bed, abandoned at birth by his HIV-infected mother. Although he wasn't ill, he had nowhere else to go. Like hundreds of other babies born to women with HIV, he became a so-called "hospital boarder baby."

Although these infants usually do not exhibit the symptoms of AIDS at birth, many live and die in a world populated only with doctors and nurses. Some have never been outdoors, according to *Time* magazine. Theirs is a hands-off existence, with little love and cuddling from mothers who, also dying of AIDS, can not or will not take care of them. Unless foster or adoptive homes can be found for them, they wind up like this child, also written about in *Time:*

> At a Harlem hospital, a boy born on Christmas four years ago lies on his back in a crib with a tube in his nose. His fingers, curled around the bottle he holds, are swollen at the ends from a lack of oxygen.
>
> Abandoned when he was six months old, the boy, suffering from a lung infection as the result of AIDS, has never known another home. There are times when he didn't need to be in the hospital, but he had nowhere else to go.[23]

Mickey was luckier. At nineteen months old, the fair-haired baby weighed only 14 pounds. *Time* magazine described the so-called "hospital-boarder baby" this way: "His huge, watchful eyes seem to fill half his face; his legs dangle like match sticks."[24] He had no visitors until Frank and Dante, a gay couple from Long Island, came along. They are the adoptive parents of two-year-old Jonathan, an AIDS baby who is blossoming under their care. They also are in the process of adopting Mickey. If the AIDS epidemic continues at its current rate, however, the number of infected children will overwhelm a foster care system already short on qualified families.

More than 400,000 children were infected with HIV worldwide by late 1990, and most were infected while in the womb, according to the World Health Organization (WHO).[25] Thirty percent will die from AIDS before they turn five; the majority will follow suit before age ten, making the disease one of the world's five leading causes of death for children from one to four years old. WHO also predicts that AIDS will spread to at least ten million children worldwide by the year 2000, and an additional ten million will have lost their parents to the disease. In the United States, researchers predict that more than twenty thousand HIV-infected children will live in the United States by the mid-1990s.[26]

The Native American community may also be struggling with extraordinary numbers of AIDS cases. In late 1992, a Navajo spokesman warned of unprecedented numbers of AIDS casualties on reservations, blaming the rampant alcoholism on reservations for widespread promiscuous sex. That has led to an AIDS epidemic on the reservations that threatens the very existence of the Navajo Nation.[27]

As the numbers of children born with HIV soar, the supply of qualified foster homes is declining. These children threaten to throw the entire system into a tailspin, prompting some to call for a new kind of orphanage in which to warehouse them. The authors believe it is imperative that these children don't grow up in such institutions.

Other Handicaps

While the nation is faced with a "new" kind of special-needs child—exposed to drugs, alcohol and HIV—it also must work with children who have more traditional challenges such as learning disabilities and physical handicaps.

Baby Olivia was born blind in a southern California hospital. Her birth parents decided they were unable to handle a child with such a severe challenge, and the social services system immediately took custody. Her parents couldn't bear to relinquish Olivia for adoption, however, so county social workers tried to find her a foster home. While they worked, Olivia spent her first few months living in a hospital ward, far longer than would have been required to treat her early handicaps.

Finally, a foster family trained to care for a child with handicaps was found, and Olivia was placed with them. Already, precious bonding time had been lost, and caseworkers weren't sure if Olivia had been psychologically damaged by the delay. They hoped the new foster parents would bond with Olivia and decide to keep her on a permanent basis.

Olivia's situation is not unusual. Children with various handicaps find themselves in the foster care system when their parents are unable to cope. Many go into small licensed family homes that are provided with extra support, specialized training and respite care. In the past, these homes have been considered the best choice for children who have:

- Learning disabilities
- Educational handicaps
- Visual impairments or blindness
- Hearing impairments or deafness
- Language disabilities
- Autism
- Multihandicaps
- Cerebral palsy
- Down's syndrome
- Neurological impairments
- Seizure disorders
- Brain tumors
- Apnea
- Medical fragility
- Mental handicaps
- Eating disorders
- Psychological handicaps

Other choices available for children with handicaps include group homes, hospital settings, treatment programs, residential care and adoptive homes. Yet, like Olivia, many are not available for adoption. Their specialized foster parents are reimbursed at a rate far higher than that for regular foster care, which may be a subtle incentive for keeping them there rather than working toward other alternatives.

Each child in foster care is also assessed for adoptability, and caseworkers determine whether a family can be found that will meet their special needs and whether the birth parents can be encouraged to relinquish. If they are found adoptable, the long, slow process begins.

The authors would like to interject an idea in which we sincerely believe: *In our opinion no child should be unadoptable.* It is important, however, that children with severe challenges are identified in the system early and given the help they need. With early intervention and proper therapy, it is possible for even the most challenged child to be adopted.

Sammy was born with cerebral palsy and is deaf. He was adopted as an infant by a couple who felt they could deal with handicaps as long as they could *actually see* them. Although he certainly wasn't the "fantasy child" they had envisioned, they wanted a child so badly they decided to stretch their expectations.

Their relationship has worked out well, but that isn't always the case with children whose handicaps are harder to see. Emotional handicaps and learning disabilities are sometimes harder to diagnose, treat and learn to cope with.

LELAND SCOVIS

Jenny and Art Scovis had no idea when three-year-old Leland arrived at their home that the child had a learning disability. When he began to have difficulties with his schoolwork, they told him he was lazy and just not working up to his potential. In some areas his scores were off the top of the charts, but in others his scores were unbelievably low.[28]

The child was also traumatized, Jenny says, "and would throw tantrums for three or four hours at a time." Eventually, his problem was diagnosed as a learning disability, probably the result of the inadequate diet he had as a baby while living in an orphanage. The Scovises found professionals who gave him educational therapy twice a week.

Not all adoptive parents are able to cope with hidden problems such as Leland's. Those who can't cope usually relinquish the child, who is then placed in a residential treatment facility or institution.

Children with Down's syndrome often go directly to state-licensed foster families as infants, and to residential facilities as adults. Some foster parents bond with their "Down's children" and end up adopting them. It often is the best solution for the children, and Social Security Insurance often pays for their basic care.

Sometimes crazy regulations interfere with what's best for a challenged child. Olivia, the blind child who spent several months in the hospital waiting for a foster home, could have been placed earlier if it wasn't for "regulations." A qualified foster home was identified outside the county in which Olivia was living, but because her birth parents had not freed her for adoption, she couldn't leave the county.

Five-year-old Abdul is in a similar situation. He lives with a foster family in Los Angeles, and hasn't seen his birth mother since he was two and a half. His foster mother, "Mary," would like to adopt him, but his birth mother won't relinquish him.

Abdul has daily periods of inconsolable screaming. During those periods, he doesn't want to be touched, and even when he is physically exhausted, he can't stop screaming. Then, suddenly, the fit is over and he becomes a loving, cuddly child. His birth mother won't admit she took drugs while carrying him, Mary says, although there is no other explanation for Abdul's behavior.[29]

Eventually, Abdul's birth mother petitioned the court to get her child back again, even though she hadn't seen him in more than two years and was suspected of abusing him *in utero*. Although Mary and her husband bonded with him, worked with his problems and paid for his therapy, the court ruled that Abdul must return to his birth mother.

The authors believe that it is difficult for many judges to understand what is "in the best interests of the children." Ignorance within the legal system is responsible for holding many children hostage when they should be free for adoption. It also is responsible for giving children back to drug-abusing birth mothers who are virtual strangers after the children have spent years with stable foster parents who would like to adopt them. Such attachment disruption is unbelievably damaging to the child.

Judges charged with making such decisions about children's lives must consider the following factors when making such important choices:

- The emotional state of the child;
- The nature of the attachment between the foster parents and the child;
- The nature of the attachment with the birth parents;
- The environment that will best match the needs of the child.[30]

Conclusions

Many of the children we've discussed are suffering the consequences of their birth parents' abuse. Some were pulled out of their birth homes and spend their numbered days in hospital wards, the equivalent of orphanages for the drug-exposed and HIV-positive babies. The foster care system and its sister, the adoption system, have not responded with a viable solution. Experts say these children need permanent placements, yet adoptive parents who are qualified and willing to take them are in short supply.

Compounding the problem, many birth parents make irresponsible choices for their children without considering the consequences. Many whose children are in foster care are reluctant to free them for adoption, and thousands of women continue to use drugs and alcohol during pregnancy. Often, it is not these people who pay the costs. It is society and the children who pay the costs.

Today, a brave few have suggested that women of childbearing age who use drugs should be required to have NORPLANT implants, birth control devices buried beneath the skin that guarantee against pregnancies for as long as five years. During that time, mothers would be encouraged to enter drug rehabilitation programs. The authors agree in theory, but only if the women are also given access to drug treatment programs.

In the meantime, we are faced with the problem of caring for the children who are already born. Several government officials have called for a return to an orphanage system for these challenged children, but we believe this is a stopgap measure that is not in the best interests of the children. The orphanage system was abandoned early in this century after institutionalized children were found to be suffering from lack of human touch and contact. The same Romanian orphanages that so appalled Americans in the early 1990s are an excellent example of those horrors.

Drug-exposed and physically handicapped children can be very difficult children to parent, but we think the answer lies in recruiting, training and supporting people willing to make the commitment. Unless we also help ourselves, we can not truly expect government programs to shoulder the entire burden of serving challenged children.

[1] Kimm Bolding, personal interview, Colorado Springs, Colorado, February 1991.

[2] General Accounting Office/Human Resources Division, *Prenatal Drug Abuse Has Increased Demand for Social Services,* June 28, 1990.

[3] General Accounting Office/Human Resources Division, *Drug-Exposed Infants,* June 28, 1990, pp. 30–31.

[4] Judy Howard, M.D., talk on special-needs adoption, Washington, DC, 1989.

[5] U.S. House Select Committee on Children, Youth and Families, Fall 1989.

[6] Judith Schaffer, North American Council on Adoptable Children 16th annual conference, Atlanta, Georgia, August, 1991.

[7] "Maria," personal interview, California, July 1991.

[8] Rep. George Miller, U.S. House Select Committee on Children, Youth and Families, Fall 1989.

[9] General Accounting Office, *Prenatal Drug Abuse.*

[10] General Accounting Office, *Drug-Exposed Infants.*

[11] hospital study, *Denver Rocky Mountain News,* September 18, 1991, p. 4.

[12] California Governor Pete Wilson, *Ventura County Star-Press,* July 19, 1991, p. C-4.

[13] General Accounting Office, *Drug-Exposed Infants.*

[14] Ira Chasnoff, M.D., NAPARE, Chicago, Illinois, 1991.

[15] Debbe Magnusen, personal interview, Costa Mesa, California, January 1991.

[16] Judy Howard, M.D., personal interview, Los Angeles, California, 1989.

[17] NAPARE, Conference Agenda bulletin, *Drug Use in Pregnancy: Impact on Families and the Growing Child,* Chicago, Illinois, April 1993.

[18] Ibid.

[19] *Congressional Update on Women,* March 31, 1992, p. 12.

[20] Ibid.

[21] Ibid.

[22] Judith Schaffer, North American Council on Adoptable Children 16th annual conference.

[23] *Time* magazine (October 9, 1990): p. 92.

[24] Ibid.

[25] "ABC News," World Health Organization, September 25, 1990.

[26] Ibid.

[27] National Public Radio, April 1992.

[28] Jenny and Art Scovis, personal interview, Camarillo, California, June 1991.

[29] "Mary," personal interview, Los Angeles, California, July 1991.

[30] Ken Magid and Carole McKelvey, *High Risk: Children Without a Conscience,* (NewYork: Bantam, 1988): p. 334.

CHAPTER EIGHT

FOREIGN ADOPTION

> *Where yet was ever found a mother,*
> *Who'd give her baby for another?*
> John Gay,
> *The Mother, the Nurse and the Fairy*

As the number of adoptable newborns falls and the demand for them by childless couples climbs, prospective American parents have turned their attention to abandoned children in other countries. In 1987, foreign children accounted for more than one of every six children adopted in the United States. About 10,100 children were adopted from eighty-three different countries, more than half (5,910) came from Korea, and another 2,000 from Central and South America.[1]

Since the federal government does not keep track of adoption figures, the National Committee for Adoption has compiled its own figures, based on data collected by the Statistical Analysis Branch, Immigration and Naturalization Service, and U.S. Department of Justice.

The figures in the latest *Adoption Factbook* show 10,097 foreign adoptees in 1987, broken down by area:

- Europe, 122
- Asia (including Korea), 7,614
- Africa, 22

- Oceania, 3
- North America, 973
- Central America, 654
- South America, 1,363

Shortly after these figures were collected, the Korean government stemmed the flood of orphans to America. By that time, more than forty thousand Korean children had been shipped abroad.

"The government has stepped up its promotion of birth control and urged Korean families to adopt," a *Time* magazine article said.[2] In 1990, the Korean government reduced by 20 percent the number of its children available for foreign adoption and initiated a model program that encouraged Korean families to adopt the unwanted children through their domestic child welfare service program.

As the major foreign source for adoptable children shrunk, Americans turned their attention to the children abandoned in Romanian orphanages and the starving victims of the Serbian-Bosnian war. Neither has proven to be a good substitute.

The appeal of foreign adoption is obvious. The process usually takes less time than an American adoption, requirements are sometimes more lenient and available babies are more plentiful. One U.S. couple applied for and received their Peruvian baby within six weeks. Other families who arrived in Romania within weeks after the country's Communist government fell came away with babies in less than six weeks.

The drawbacks are not as obvious—bureaucratic red tape, corruption and children with hidden physical or mental problems. One family who adopted a neglected, ill child from a Romanian orphanage discovered that she was deaf. That adoption eventually failed because the family didn't have the resources to cope with her challenges.

Their example is not unique. Consider the case of "John," a twelve-year-old Korean orphan adopted by an American couple.

John

The last few weeks that John lived with his adoptive parents in Colorado, they slept with bells tied to their bedroom door. They were afraid he would murder them in the night.

After more than a year in their home, the fourteen-year-old Korean boy had driven his adopted mother to the brink of a nervous breakdown, alienated his adopted father and terrorized his adopted sister. Nevertheless, they agonized over the decision to give him back to the adoption agency. In the end, they had no choice. They were afraid they had unknowingly welcomed a psychopath into their home.

Family members blame themselves for the adoption failure. Privately, they also blame the adoption agency that helped them bring John to the United States. They say the agency gave them too little information about the boy and too little support once his problems became apparent. The medical papers they received said nothing was wrong with the boy. The truth was apparent almost immediately after he stepped off the plane from Korea.

John was their second Korean-born child. Kim, age sixteen, was the first. She adjusted well to her new parents and remains with the family. But John was different. "For the next one and a half years, we had not one good day," his mother says, listing a string of horrifying incidents. She says John:

- Told his adopted sister he wanted her dead;
- Threatened his mother with violence;
- Was cruel to animals;
- Tore things to shreds just for spite;
- Beat up and hurt children in school, interrupting classes; and
- Disrupted family activities when they went on vacations.

At one point, his mother pleaded with the adoption agency for help, asking, "What do I have in my home, a Ted Bundy?" The family insists the private adoption agency gave them no support and sometimes didn't even return their phone calls.

They say John was severely ill when he arrived on the plane, "so weak and thin, and his skin was jaundiced," his mother remembers. "His teeth were so badly abscessed we had to get him to a dentist immediately." They also discovered John had hepatitis B, an extremely contagious and incurable disease usually detected in the immigration process. Persons diagnosed with the disease are not admitted into the United States. When they notified the adoption agency, however, they were told, "Don't tell anyone! He will be even more discriminated against," the mother says.

Hepatitis B is a viral infection that is more common in Asian and African countries than in the United States. It is a progressive disease that attacks the liver and affects its function. To prevent its spread, uninfected family members must minimize contact with blood and avoid sharing toothbrushes and other items that come in contact with the gums. It is unknown how many potential adoptees from foreign nations carry hepatitis B, but theoretically these children, like those with HIV, should not pass the admission requirements for immigration into the United States. A simple blood test can detect the disease, but for some reason, John's case was not detected. John's case was brought under control slowly, through a regular diet and other treatments, but it wasn't the worst ordeal his adopted family would face. John had trouble with schoolwork, was extremely disruptive and sometimes became violent.

John's mother says she dreaded having the phone ring because school officials called so often to report the boy's bad behavior. Once they called to say that John had grabbed the breasts of eight girls. Another schoolmate complained that John threw him against a fence, threw rocks at him and beat him up. Teachers also reported that John was functionally illiterate, even in his native Korean, although adoption reports indicated he had attended school.

Animals also knew instinctively that John would hurt them and went berserk when he approached, according to his mother. "They often barked and cried and ran away," she says. "Any dog he could get to was greeted with a kick."

Eventually the family consulted experts. They were told the boy was dangerous and were advised to get him out of the house as quickly as possible. They held out until one day John and his mother were home alone together. She told him to do something he didn't want to do. He glared at her with what she describes as a demonic look.

"His eyes just turned black, and he stared and stared at me," she says. "Then he flung his chair aside and came at me, his hands in a strangle-type hold. I became really frightened, realizing he was almost as big as me now. I wasn't sure I would be able to fight him off."

She managed to stare him down, but he turned his anger from her to household items. He rampaged through the house, throwing and smashing things. That day she realized they needed help, but none was forthcoming from the adoption agency. The family's calls weren't returned.

In January, 1988, they ordered their attorney to stop the adoption and to return John to the agency. Psychologists say that John was "acting out" because of trauma in his early life and that John was unable to love or attach to this American family. The failed adoption and John's medical bills cost them more than $10,000.

How to Decide

Many foreign adoptions work out better than John's, especially when the children are young and well matched to their adoptive families' personalities, temperaments and cultural backgrounds. All adopted children come with histories of pain and loss, but foreign children must also deal with the loss of their native culture and language.

To help people considering foreign adoptions, the International Concerns Committee for Children (ICCC) has published a list of characteristics typical of older children adopted from foreign countries, as compared to older American children waiting for adoption:

CHARACTERISTICS OF ADOPTED CHILDREN

Incountry	Intercountry
1. Basic nutrition needs satisfied	1. Food restricted, undernourished
2. Poor	2. Often extreme poverty
3. Schooling of some sort	3. Little or no schooling
4. Usually mandated review of status	4. Caste system; orphans socially unacceptable
5. Necessary/advisable medical care	5. Little or no care
6. Foster care	6. Few material comforts
7. Result: invisible institution	7. Result: street life or visible institution
8. Isolated from family (unless siblings placed together)	8. Part of a group, not biologically related

9. Self-centered	9. Has learned to share
10. Trouble with relationships	10. Understands inter-dependence
11. Manipulative	11. May help others
12. Handicapping conditions being aided	12. Little or no aid available
13. Relative physical peace	13. Often physical conflict
14. Often emotionally troubled	14. Emotional stability[3]

The agency urges parents to think carefully about their ability to work with foreign children. It also recommends screening potential adoption agencies before working with one. Parents should ask for references and talk to others who have had experience with them, especially about the kind of support and follow-up that is provided. Regional adoption exchanges also may have information about the agency's reputation.

Once the decision has been made to pursue a foreign adoption and an agency has been selected, ICCC suggests that parents demand information about:

- The child's medical, mental and genetic history;
- Why the child was given up for adoption (orphaned, poverty, culture, illness, abandonment)and why another relative didn't take the child in; and
- The culture of the child's native country. Find out about religious background and cultural mores, then decide if they are things that can be accommodated.

Couples who adopt foreign children will have to consider how they will feel if the child does not resemble them or is attached to a foreign religion or celebrates customs that are unfamiliar and is thus discriminated against. Many of the children available for adoption in Eastern European countries, for example, are descended from gypsies and are considered social outcasts in their own countries. They have known discrimination and deprivation as a result.

Finding an agency that specializes in the part of the world you are interested in also can be very helpful. Some specialize in children from Latin American countries, others in children from Asia or Europe.

A comprehensive listing of agencies and countries they are familiar with, called the *Report on Foreign Adoption, 1993,* is available from International Concerns Committee for Children.

THE DEPRIVED CHILD

- Prognosis is uncertain. Yet the human spirit is resilient; many children thrive when given opportunities to love and explore.
- Weight size and development do not progress as with family children.
- Speech is delayed.
- With no one to rock them, they sit and rock themselves or engage in other self-stimulation.
- If there is no one to answer a cry, the child learns not to call. If they do not bond with another person, social and emotional problems are likely.
- If their movement has been restrained, their muscles atrophy and spirits become forlorn.
- They are malnourished and many have medical problems (e.g., rickets, hepatitis B). Many test positive for HIV and AIDS.

Although children of war are particularly traumatized, they are also the ones who tug on the heartstrings of well-meaning Americans. When the faces of war-ravaged orphans begin appearing on television or in the newspapers, adoption agencies brace themselves for a barrage of phone calls.

It happened in late 1992 and early 1993, when the faces of crying orphans from the Bosnian-Serbian conflict saturated the media. American couples, eager to rescue the children, flooded the State Department and adoption agencies with calls.

"It's like a feeding frenzy, and I blame the media for whipping it up," said Ann Marie Merrill of the Colorado-based ICCC. "I've had several people who want to adopt tell me they were ready to get on a plane. People see pictures of hurt children, and it brings out the savior complex in them."[4]

In August, 1992, the U.S. Department of State put this message on an adoption hotline operated by its Office of Citizens' Consular

Services: "The Department of State strongly advises U.S. citizens no to attempt adoptions in the former Yugoslavia at this time."[5] Its advisory was still in effect in 1993.

Like many war-worn countries, the former Yugoslavian nation is a poor prospect for adoptions for several reasons. Many of the children listed as orphans are merely separated from their families by the conflict. Plus, such countries usually have no history of international adoption and will allow it only if one of the adopting parents is a native of the country.

Romanian Children

Americans learned a hard lesson in 1990, when they saw television reports of orphans left behind when Romanian dictator Nicolae Ceausescu was overthrown. Hundreds rushed to adopt the children, but the fledgling government did not have the systems in place to handle the crush of foreign interest. Eventually, it put a moratorium on adoptions until it developed an adequate system in 1993.

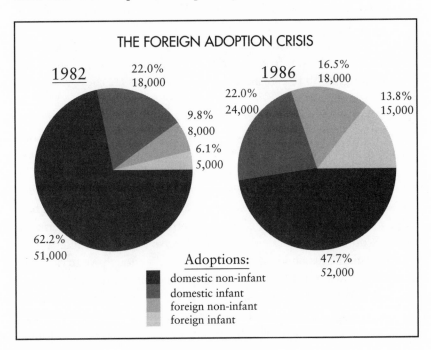

THE FOREIGN ADOPTION CRISIS

1982

22.0% 18,000
9.8% 8,000
6.1% 5,000
62.2% 51,000

1986

16.5% 18,000
22.0% 24,000
13.8% 15,000
47.7% 52,000

Adoptions:
domestic non-infant
domestic infant
foreign non-infant
foreign infant

In the meantime, nearly 100,000 orphans languished in the country's seventy-eight state-run orphanages, the result of Ceausescu's mandatory fertility policy. For twenty-four years, the Communist ruler had required all Romanian women of childbearing age to have at least five children. His goal was to increase his country's population from 23 million to 30 million by the year 2000, thereby swelling its labor pool.

His plan was dismantled by the harsh realities of life in Communist Romania. Because of poor nutrition, inadequate prenatal care and birth defects, the country's orphanages were filled with children who were handicapped or whose families couldn't support them.

Ceausescu began the campaign in 1966 with this proclamation: "The fetus is the property of the entire society. Anyone who avoids having children is a deserter who abandons the laws of national continuity."[6]

All contraception was banned, and abortion was outlawed. Factory workers were subjected to periodic mandatory pregnancy tests to prevent clandestine abortions. The logic was straightforward. "The more Romanians there are, the more soldiers," says Ilona Scott of Camarillo, California, a Romanian refugee who later adopted a child from Romania. "More workers, servants, security police or whatever. The rumors are that most of [Ceausescu's] elite security police were populations from the orphanages, raised especially for him. They felt so grateful to [be] alive ... they did whatever they were told to do."[7]

Not all children were lucky enough to join Ceausescu's forces. Many died at birth. (The infant mortality rate rose to eighty-three deaths per one thousand births, compared to less than ten deaths per one thousand births in Western Europe.)[8] Of the babies that did survive, one in ten was born underweight. Newborns weighing as little as 3 pounds, 5 ounces were classified as miscarriages and denied treatment. They ended up in the orphanages, along with other unwanted children and babies. Scott notes: "Children's mortality was so high that to hide it they would not name the children until they were old enough to survive. So, there were thousands of children who died without a name."

Scott grew up in Romania, but married an American man, Toby Scott, and immigrated to America seventeen years ago. It took Ceausescu a year and a half to sign her emigration papers. Ironically, she found herself waiting for Romanian signatures again when she and Toby tried to adopt a child from one of the state-run orphanages in 1985.

"We went there to adopt, with all the papers in order," Scott says. "I had a notion that I had to get another soul out of that misery. I didn't know what misery was until I got back there."

Adopting in Romania turned out to be harder than the Scotts imagined. Their child, a nine-month-old girl named Jessica, was preselected for them by a lawyer. He had several more children in reserve in case they didn't like her. That wasn't necessary.

Scott says she knew Jessica was the child for them the instant she held her, even though the child initially showed no response to being held. "She only answered for hunger. While we were holding her, she got hungry and started to scream. They brought a bottle. We fed her. She laid back," says Scott. "But we played with her. Toby wanted to see if she could crawl. She would crawl. She would keep her head up."

Eventually they were rewarded for their perseverance. Jessica grew to expect their visits, and when they took her to a park one day, they were rewarded with "a very funny, husky kind of laugh." The Scotts weren't able to accelerate the paperwork, however, and after two weeks they returned to California without Jessica. While waiting three and a half years for the bureaucracy to process their adoption application, they paid Romanians to visit Jessica in the orphanage.

"There were people coming for her, paid by us, bringing things to her that she could give to others," Scott says. "She was the center of attention. She was getting chocolates, toys." The paid visitors also took her on walks and gave her pictures of the Scotts to kiss and hold. Without this extra attention, the couple believes, she wouldn't have flourished as she has.

The revolution of 1989–90 was the opportunity they had been waiting for, Scott says. They arrived in Romania just as the revolution was ending and claimed their now four-year-old adoptive daughter, who had been spirited out of the institution by people who claimed they were related to her.

Now living with the couple in southern California, Jessica speaks English, although she and Ilona occasionally lapse into Romanian. Scott noted that Jessica often refuses to speak her native language, probably because most of the child's bad memories are connected with that language. By conversing with her in her native tongue, however, Scott says she has been able to unlock some of the memories and help the child adjust.

Today, Jessica makes up stories about her past, talking about the bad man who wouldn't let her out and the "dirty house with no pillows" (the orphanage). Scott assures her she won't ever have to go back to the "dirty house."

Scott also spent weeks convincing Jessica that she would always have food. At first, the child hoarded food and wet her pants at the table rather than leave her food behind. She was afraid the food would be taken away while she was gone.

Despite Jessica's early deprivation, Scott feels the child is "very, very whole," and they have been remarkably lucky. Westerners who witnessed the conditions at state-run orphanages would agree. Observers who visited the orphanages after Ceausescu's overthrow found babies in cold rooms, bundled up in sweaters and caps and sitting blank-faced. Forced to comfort themselves, some rocked themselves all day.

"There they were, all in their little nightgowns in their iron cribs, lying quietly, rocking themselves," said Dr. Barbara Bascom of World Vision's Romanian Orphans Social and Education Support Project (ROSES). She toured seventeen of Romania's orphanages in 1990. "Most of these children wouldn't reach for you, and some recoiled when we tried to touch them."[9] Bascom said she feared for the babies' futures, wondering how they ever would catch up developmentally if they managed to get out of the orphanages.

Associated Press journalist Edie Lederer reported on overworked orphanage employees—sometimes only one or two to care for hundreds of babies—who had all they could do to feed the children. She told delegates to the 1990 JAWS Conference in Santa Fe, New Mexico, that even the children's rations were meager, the equivalent of about 25 cents worth of food a day.[10]

Dixie van de Flier Davis of the Rocky Mountain Adoption Exchange traveled to Romania several times between mid-1990 and 1991 to help assess the situation there. She was appalled to find baby-selling in the lobby of the Intercontinental Hotel in Bucharest. "Taxi drivers said to you, 'Well, I can take you to a family.' I am afraid that all kinds of things are going to happen," she said.

"I think there are probably going to be some not so pretty legal complications one of these days," she said at the time, " ... where money has changed hands for relinquishment of a child that wasn't even their child ... I mean, don't you think that is possible in that kind of crazy system?"[11]

Reporters on the television news show "20/20" told viewers about Romanian birth parents who were demanding and receiving more than $5,000 in exchange for relinquishing their babies. One father demanded $10,000 plus a car in exchange for his newborn son.

The early moratorium on adoptions ended that, but Davis and the Adoption Exchange have stayed active, helping to train Romanian adoption workers and consulting with Romanian officials on a program to care for its own handicapped children. As in America, the country's older handicapped children are the last to find permanent homes.

One American family felt an almost "indescribable pull" toward such a child when they saw her story in *People* magazine. Greti and Rick Dorr of Cincinnati first saw a picture of Adriana in the January, 1991, article and knew instantly she was the one for them. Greti flew to the child's Bucharest orphanage four months later, and returned with Adriana in July. She joined two biological children, Elizabeth and Ben.

Though the three-year-old child arrived with deformed hands and club feet, the couple doesn't care, they told *People*.[12] Those handicaps "only made her more precious," Greti said.

South American Children

In the 1980s, many American couples interested in adopting turned to South and Central America for help. In 1986 and 1987 alone, more than two thousand South and Central American babies made their way to families in the United States.

Some of the adoptive parents, particularly those living in southwestern states, were enamored with American Indian culture, according to a former social worker now living in Albuquerque, New Mexico. Other couples wanted "babies with a little history or roots behind them," she added. "Most Americans don't have that connection."

They began importing babies from their neighbors to the south. South and Central American babies comprise the second largest group of foreign babies adopted by American couples, according to the *Adoption Factbook*.[13]

But without a strong body regulating the adoptions, abuses began to occur, including "baby trafficking." One well-publicized case in Galveston, Texas, revolved around a jailed Hispanic prostitute who was charged with selling her four multicultural babies and the Galveston adoption attorney who allegedly bought them and placed them with U.S. families. The attorney's child-placement license eventually was revoked, but only after all four of the woman's babies had been adopted.

According to reports in the *Houston Chronicle,* Adamina De Jesus had seven children, none of whom she was raising herself.[14] Relatives and friends said the prostitute turned three of the children over to them and sold the other four to attorney Leslie Thacker. Thacker denied the claims.

Family members also accused De Jesus of using drugs while pregnant with some of the children. The woman was serving a six-year sentence for vehicle burglary when she first met Thacker, and her arrest record shows convictions for intravenous drug use, prostitution and theft. Relatives of De Jesus said they first heard of seventy-three-year-old Thacker when Adamina got an early release from jail in early 1990. Thacker allegedly had paid a Galveston bondsman $650 to post bail.

Juanita Medrano, a friend who is raising De Jesus' six-year-old daughter "Little Adamina," said the woman told her she met Thacker over the phone through one of the inmates. "She said she wants to buy my babies," De Jesus told her. "This lady has a lot of money. She is my lawyer friend."

Thacker allegedly waited for Adamina in her car outside Medrano's home while the two women talked. Medrano recalled her friend saying, "You see that old lady out there in the black Cadillac? I'm going to use her. She paid for me to get out because she wants these kids real bad."[15]

Thacker testified in June, 1990, that she was involved in the exchange of 750 babies through adoption. She told the court she charged U.S. parents $11,000 for each child, more than twice the average fee of $5,204 paid to member agencies of the National Committee for Adoption.

The abuses weren't detected earlier, according to the *Chronicle*, because "court records are sealed in most adoption cases." The De Jesus case, fought in open court, gave the public "a rare glimpse into the secretive world of adoption," wrote reporter Steven Long. "Although secrecy is generally believed to protect the child, in some cases it may be used as a shield for shady practices. The De Jesus case has been a frightening look behind that shield."

Conclusions

Many Americans who are hungry for a child of their own are willing to go to the ends of the earth to find one. Some have but one thing in mind—coming home with a healthy baby—and they are willing to "buy" one if they have to. Even legal foreign adoptions can be difficult and problem-filled.

If a couple decides to adopt a foreign child, adoption officials feel it is wise to check first with the U.S. Immigration Service and the Department of State to get the required paperwork underway. They should also be prepared for bureaucratic messes, with delays and bribes being the norm. Perhaps the safest route to a foreign child is through one of the many U.S. adoption agencies now operating on foreign soil.

We must consider the moral dilemma that comes into play when Americans comb the world for adoptable infants while a growing number of special-needs children remain in limbo in America. The dilemma: Do we try to encourage families to adopt them, or do we encourage them to rescue children from the Third World?

It has been the authors' stand that Americans need to adopt American children before they look outside of U.S. borders. Adoptive parents must make this decision themselves, however, and not allow others to push them into parenting a child they are unprepared for. In the end, it should be the right of every child, regardless of nationality, to have a family.

---

[1] National Committee for Adoption, *Adoption Factbook*, 1989, p. 101.

[2] *Time* magazine (October 9, 1989).

[3] International Concerns Committee for Children, *Report on Foreign Adoption*, 1993.

[4] *Denver Rocky Mountain News,* August 5, 1992, p. 156.

[5] Ibid.

[6] *Newsweek* (January 22, 1990): p. 35.

[7] Ilona and Toby Scott, personal interview, southern California, Summer 1990.

[8] *Newsweek* (January 22, 1990): p. 35.

[9] Barbara Bascom, Romanian Orphans Social and Education Support Project (ROSES), press release, 1990.

[10] Edie Lederer, Journalism and Women's Symposium (JAWS), September 1990.

[11] Dixie van de Flier Davis, personal interview, Denver, Colorado, Summer 1991.

[12] Greti and Rick Dorr, quoted in *People* magazine (January 1991): pp. 13–15.

[13] National Committee for Adoption, *Adoption Factbook,* 1989.

[14] Steven Long, *Houston Chronicle,* October 21, 1990, p. 1G.

[15] Ibid.

THE RESEARCH

CHAPTER NINE

THE GENETIC INFLUENCE

*To forget one's ancestors is to be
a brook without a source,
a tree without a root.*
Chinese Proverb

For decades, experts taught that nurturing parents and a positive environment made all the difference in a child's life—that *nurture* was a more important influence than *nature*.

While not discounting the importance of good parents, new researchers are finding that nature may be the stronger influence of the two. They are finding evidence that the traits passed down on the twisted spirals of DNA can play "a remarkably powerful role in the development of a child's personality."[1]

Nature versus Nurture

Researchers at universities and medical facilities across the country are discovering that, like black hair or dark complexions, children's personalities are at least in part inherited. Their findings suggest that children are predisposed to possessing their parents' traits and temperaments.

Parents always have had a hunch that that was the case, recognizing that their children not only look like them but act like them, too. It's not uncommon to hear parents say things like, "She is sloppy, just like you," or "He takes after his mother, he's very smart."

"Babies have different personalities, if not from day one then from day two," child psychologist Irene Chatoor told a *Child* magazine reporter. "Parents feel it, and now the professionals are confirming those instincts."[2]

TWIN STUDIES

Jim Lewis and Jim Springer, fifty-year-old identical twins, were separated at birth and brought together only as adults by the University of Minnesota's Twins Project. The two men had similar personalities, drove identical cars, smoked the same brand of cigarettes, vacationed in the same Florida town and had dogs named "Toy."[3]

Amazing? No, genetics. Other studies have shown that separated identical twins often share similar personality profiles, even walking alike, talking alike and sitting in chairs the same way. Researchers also find that twins grow more alike as they get older.

HEREDITARY TRAITS

The personality traits researchers now think are hereditary include shyness, resilience, self-confidence, intelligence and attention span. Decades of work with infants, twins and parents around the world have come together to provide evidence for these theories, including the research of:

- Dr. Jerome Kagan, a child psychologist at Harvard who is an authority on genetics. He confirmed the theory that shyness is innate and appears during the toddler years.
- Thomas J. Bouchard, Jr., and his colleagues at the University of Minnesota, Minneapolis. They find that identical twins raised in different households are almost as similar in personality and intelligence as identical twins who are raised together.

- Adam Matheny, a psychologist at the University of Louisville. He has found that intelligence is hereditary.
- Robert Plomin, a researcher at Pennsylvania State University's College of Health and Human Development. He is studying the genetic link to personality, attitudes and beliefs.
- Umea University Medical School in Sweden. Researchers have found direct ties between alcoholic parents and children who are alcoholic, or who suffer from psychosomatic illness or engage in criminal acts.
- Richard Olson and Barbara Wise, researchers at the University of Colorado at Boulder's Institute for Behavioral Genetics. They find evidence that dyslexia has a genetic link.

In his study of identical twins raised apart, Bouchard administered IQ tests and interviewed his subjects about life history, psychiatric history and sexual life history. He also examined environmental factors, including socioeconomic status indicators; parents' education; father's socioeconomic status; material possessions; and scientific/technical, cultural and mechanical resources.

Bouchard's team also gave study subjects the Moos Family Environment Scale, a tool that describes an individual's adult impression of treatment and rearing by adoptive parents during childhood and adolescence, and he considered the amount of contact the twins had with each other before and after their separation. Identical twins reared apart were compared with identical twins raised together, and both were compared with fraternal twins.

In all, more than one hundred twins participated. From the data, Bouchard drew the following conclusions about the effects of environment and genetics:

- General intelligence, or IQ, is strongly affected by genetic factors, although it may be enhanced by optimal environment.
- The institutions and practices of modern Western society do not greatly constrain the development of individual differences in psychological traits. People develop according to their genetic individual differences, and family rearing doesn't change that a whole lot.

- Identical twins reared apart are so similar in psychological traits because their identical genes make it probable they will get similar responses from the people around them. For example, it is well documented that toddlers who are active and adventurous have different experiences than their more sedentary or timid siblings. In addition, children and adolescents seek environments that are favorable for them.
- Genes for IQ and personality probably work indirectly, affecting the way people react to their experiences and the choices they have made.

The implication of this study is that "the correct formula is nature *via* nurture," which means that most inherited traits can be mediated through intervention, especially when it is "tailored to each specific child's talents and inclinations," Bouchard writes in *Science* magazine.[4]

"For almost every behavioral trait so far investigated, from reaction to religiosity, an important fraction of the variation among people turns out to be associated with genetic variation," Bouchard concludes. "This fact need no longer be subject to debate."[5]

The study found that twins raised by the same parents were no more alike than twins raised separately. The remarkably similar social attitudes of twins reared apart, Bouchard writes, "do not show that parents can not influence those traits, but simply that this does not tend to happen in most families."[6]

Adam Matheny's research at the University of Louisville has revealed strong indications that intelligence is inherited. Because of the social implications, his findings tend to make people edgy, he says, but adds, "the public needs to be educated."[7] His research makes it apparent that good parenting, education and other interventions are still effective in boosting children's rates of learning, the authors add, but they may have little influence over the ultimate levels attained.

Robert Plomin has highlighted genetic research showing a hereditary link between such characteristics and illnesses as:

- Intellectual factors, such as specific cognitive abilities, academic achievement, reading disability and mental retardation;

- Personality factors, including extroversion, neuroticism, temperament in childhood, attitudes and beliefs;
- Psychopathology, such as schizophrenia, affective disorders, delinquent and criminal behavior and alcoholism.[8]

Plomin cites two long-term studies of the genetic influence on intelligence quotient (IQ) scores—the Louisville Twin Study (1983) and the Colorado Adoption Project (1988). "Results of these two studies indicate that genetic influence on IQ increases substantially during childhood," Plomin writes, also affecting academic achievement and reading disability, as well as mental retardation.[9]

Studies by Richard Olson and Barbara Wise at the University of Colorado in Boulder are finding strong evidence of a genetic factor behind dyslexia, which causes reading disabilities. The researchers, in collaboration with John DeFries and David Fulker of the Institute for Behavioral Genetics, have been conducting experiments since 1982 that compare identical and fraternal same-sex twins.

They have looked at cases in which one twin is diagnosed as reading disabled and theorized that, if dyslexia is an inherited problem, the identical twin should also be dyslexic. After studying more than two hundred twins, they see the clear presence of such a genetic tie.[10]

PERSONALITY FACTORS

Some recent research has focused on two "super factors" of personality: extroversion and neuroticism. Research involving more than twenty-five thousand twins showed heritability estimates of about 50 percent for these two traits.[11]

After carefully examining adopted children involved in the longitudinal study of the Colorado Adoption Project, Plomin said he is studying the possibility that personality is, indeed, inherited. He believes that the evidence increases as the individual ages, which explains why separated twins get more and more alike as they get older.[12]

This is a dramatic breakthrough in the study of personality development. These studies have found, for example, that sociability is at the core of extroversion, and emotionality is the major component of neuroticism. Both traits—sociability and emotionality—are among the most inherited of personality factors. Many personality traits, therefore, can be considered to display genetic influences.

Another example is traditionalism, defined as "the tendency to follow rules and authority and endorse high moral standards and strict discipline." Plomin cites one large twin study that found that half the influence for this tendency was inherited.[13]

Lauren's Story

"Lauren Steel" got off to a bumpy start in life, spending her first two weeks with foster parents who didn't give her much nurturing. But more troubling than her reluctance to bond was her inborn personality. She was extroverted and emotional; her adoptive parents, both mental health professionals, were quiet, passive and introverted.

For a long time, Lauren was an embarrassment to her adoptive father, who taught others how to raise their children but could not cope with this child. Lauren threw screaming fits at home and in public. She wouldn't listen and was terribly afraid of people. "She was ... just super active, if not hyperactive," says adoptive mother "Joan Steel."[14]

These knowledgeable, educated adoptive parents did everything they could think of to understand where Lauren was coming from. Their efforts seem to have paid off, as today this child is a healthy, happy adult who is succeeding in college and is close to her parents and sister.

While undergoing her own therapy in later years, however, Joan says, "Lauren was the focus of a lot of my sessions. [Since she was adopted], it was a little easier for me to accept the way she was, because I didn't have to blame myself or feel guilty for the genes I had passed on to her. I truly liked who she was, despite the problems."

Psychopathology

Some inherited personality traits lead to disorders such as schizophrenia, affective disorders, delinquent and criminal behavior and alcoholism. Twin studies have shown that, if one of two identical twins is schizophrenic, the other is eight times more likely than the general population to develop the same disorder.

A genetic link to manic-depressive illness has also been found. This illness affects the offspring of identical twins, regardless of whether the twin was manic-depressive. The dominant gene "Chromosome 11" is a main link to manic-depressive illness.

Called "genetic markers," these dominant genes are like road maps to the human condition. Since the first gene for Huntington's Disease was discovered on "Chromosome 4" in 1983, researchers have attempted to map the functions of human chromosomes. Other psychopathologies that have shown genetic influence include panic disorder and anorexia nervosa, and several groups are attempting to prove that juvenile delinquents who go on to become adult criminals have a genetic predisposition.[15]

Alcoholism

Scientists feel they are hot on the trail of a genetic chromosome marker for alcoholism, which would prove that the predisposition for alcoholism does run in families. Studies show that about 25 percent of the male relatives of alcoholics also are alcoholic, as are 22 percent of the sons of alcoholics who have been raised by adoptive parents. (Incidence of alcoholism in the general population is less than 5 percent.)[16]

In one study, University of Wyoming researchers found that children of alcoholic families are more likely to develop alcoholism or other compulsive behaviors than children of nonalcoholics. Marylou Scavnicky-Mylant, an associate professor, studied children of alcoholics for a genetic and behavioral tendency toward addiction. She found that young adult children of alcoholics are slower to develop problem-solving techniques than the general population, which results in arrested development.[17]

THE SWEDISH STUDY

Further evidence of the genetic ties to alcoholism continue to come from a ground-breaking long-term Swedish study, in which hundreds of adoptees have been tracked over a lifetime. Researchers at the Umea University Medical School in Stockholm have found direct ties, for example, between the sons and daughters of alcoholic fathers who then exhibit this behavior themselves.

Dr. C. Robert Cloninger, a psychiatrist and population geneticist at Washington University in St. Louis, Missouri, has been participating in the study. He calls the Swedish study "a marvelous laboratory" because most people in Sweden are of the same ethnic background, and because extreme wealth and extreme poverty are rare. These facts make genetic factors stand out more clearly than in the United States, with its more diverse ethnic, racial and social populations.[18]

The Swedish researchers have access to the records of 1,775 adopted men and women born between 1930 and 1949, as well as the records of their biological and adoptive parents. Factors emerging from their records include:

- *Alcohol abuse.* Of the 1,775 adoptees, alcoholism was a problem for 300, two-thirds of them men. Two types of alcoholism were identified. The first, found only in men, involved severe drinking problems that developed in the teen years, leading to alcohol-related and often violent misdeeds. Researchers found that 18 percent were the biological sons of alcoholic men.

  The second type, found in men and women, involved mild to moderate drinking problems. These children developed drinking problems even in "good" adoptive homes, but their alcoholism was severe if their adoptive parents were heavy drinkers. Researchers concluded that their environment exacerbated a genetic predisposition.

- *Psychosomatic illness.* Researchers wondered why only men developed the first type of alcohol abuse, and why men were five to six times more likely to be alcoholic than women. While studying the adopted children's records, they stumbled onto another fact—that women inherited the same genetic weakness but manifested it differently. They found in the health and employment records of adopted women, for example, that one group had numerous sick leaves, often for such ailments as stomachaches or other vague pains. One female adoptee with fine health in childhood had a record of forty-seven sick leaves from her secretarial position by age thirty-three. She had been diagnosed as having "generalized anxiety disorder."[19]

Researchers discovered that 23 percent of the women who took excessive sick leave had biological fathers who were alcoholic. They concluded that "whatever predisposed the sons of these severely alcoholic fathers to alcoholism was also making the daughters more likely to suffer psychosomatic illnesses."[20]

■ *Criminality.* The Swedish researchers also looked at the link to criminality, although they were cautious about this controversial issue. Again, they discovered patterns suggesting the impact of both heredity and the environment. They found that

1. Adopted men who grew up in "good" adoptive families and whose biological parents were law-abiding had only a 3 percent conviction rate;
2. Men raised in "good" homes whose biological parents had been convicted of crimes had a 12 percent conviction rate (this group may provide evidence that a good environment can help overcome a genetic predisposition to crime); and
3. Men whose biological parents had criminal records and whose adoptive homes weren't ideal had a 40 percent conviction rate.

Combining Nature and Nurture

The authors feel it is important to point out something that behavioral genetic research shows clearly—that human development depends on both nature and nurture. In other words, an individual may inherit the predisposition toward a behavior, but does not necessarily have to follow through. Only certain things about a child can be changed, but it is possible for good adoptive parents to steer a youngster away from traits that may lead to trouble.

At the same time, it is critical that scientists weigh the ramifications of their future study results. For example, how will future societies use the science of genetics to predict criminal or antisocial behavior? What will happen to the adoption and the reproduction processes?

A recent issue of *Caring*, the official publication of the National Association of Homes for Children, warns of the implications. "Will certain persons be 'labeled' at birth? How will children coming into care be screened [for] future placement and estimate[s made] of lifetime success or failure?"[21]

Genetics and Clinicians

Dr. Foster Cline of Colorado is an internationally known psychiatrist who treats extremely disturbed children. Many of them are adopted children who suffered bonding breaks early in life. The more he studies troubled children, the more he feels genetics play "a major role" in their outcome.

Cline pioneered a treatment for attachment-disordered children that is known as Rage Reduction Therapy. He is also a founder of the Youth Behavior Program, Evergreen Consultants in Human Behavior and the Attachment Center at Evergreen, Colorado. He and his wife, Hermie, have three birth children and an adopted daughter, now fifteen.

Cline says it is easy to see why discussions about genetics make some adoption workers uneasy. Does it mean adoptive parents have no effect on the children they are trying to love and raise? Cline says no. "What we are really trying to do is have responsible folks with responsible genes raise the offspring of parents with what we might call 'fragile genes',," he explains.

By "fragile genes" he means a genetic predisposition for intelligence deficits or psychopathology. Others use the terms "dysfunctional families," "poor genetics," "uneven genetics," "lumpy genetics" and "uneven temperament" to describe the same thing.

"The birth parents may have had fragile genetics, and then they add to that by drinking during pregnancy or doing other drugs," Cline says. As if the fragile genetics aren't bad enough, parents who give their children a poor first year can doom them to a life of misery.

"What results are very disturbed children with numerous problems," Cline says. "Then we put these kids from very irresponsible families and circumstances into [families] that expect to make them into responsible adults."[22] Unless the adoptive parents understand the child's genetic history and early life experiences, they will never succeed.

By identifying a child's genetic predisposition, for example, parents can provide the best possible environment for keeping "pit-bull kids" from nipping at their "collie" parents' heels. As one adoptive mother said in late 1991: "We knew in advance what we were taking on. It isn't his fault. We just feel our son needs a chance, and we're giving him that chance."

SPEAKING GENETIC "LANGUAGE"

Just what is a genetic disorder? *Genetic* means *"of the genes."* The four basic types of genetic disorders include:

- *Single gene.* The basic units of inheritance, with everyone having genes that could result in disease or handicap. Sometimes the disorder is seen in every generation of a family, other times there is no known family history of the condition, and in still other cases, the condition is seen only in boys.

- *Chromosomal.* Genes carried on "packages" called chromosomes. It is possible for an accident to occur at conception resulting in incorrect numbers of chromosomes, or misshapen structures. This can happen to any child, but most chromosome accidents result in an early spontaneous abortion, stillbirth or death shortly after birth.[23] A case in which death does not always happen is Down's syndrome, a common cause of mental retardation, which is a chromosomal disorder.

- *Environmentally induced.* A genetic disorder caused by exposure to environmental agents that can cause birth defects. Fetal alcohol syndrome is an example. Some hyperactive children, or those who have difficulty concentrating or display poor impulse control, may be suffering from the effects of fetal alcohol exposure. Other ways a baby may be harmed before birth include recreational drugs, over-the-counter and prescribed medicines, radiation, viral infections, including sexually transmitted diseases, and stress to the mother. That includes babies born to mothers infected with HIV. Environmental factors can harm genes or interfere with genetic processes after birth, including causing certain types of cancer.

- *Interaction of genetic vulnerability and environmental factors.* When genetic combinations and the environment interact, such things as abnormal height and weight of the baby can result. Other birth defects are caused by this kind of interaction, including cleft lip, cleft palate and spina bifida.

Getting Genetic Help for Medical Problems

How, then, do people find genetic answers and help? *Adoption Worker's Guide to Genetic Services,* a booklet by Julia B. Rauch and Nancy Rike of the University of Maryland, School of Social Work and Community Planning, focuses on genetic abnormalities. It is distributed by the National Resource Center for Special Needs Adoption in Chelsea, Michigan.

It discusses birth defects, and covers the development of medical problems as the child grows. It also answers the question, "Why are genetic services relevant to adoptions?" and urges adoption workers to identify adoptees who should be evaluated by a medical geneticist. These questions are particularly relevant to infants born drug-exposed.

"Health in adulthood may also be promoted if genetic information is available to the adoptee," they write.[24] This is especially true when dealing with an inherited predisposition for such diseases as cardiovascular disorders, cancer, diabetes and some senile dementias. With this kind of genetic information, persons with a predisposition can take steps to reduce the risk and receive early treatment.

What genetic services are available to discover medical problems? Throughout the nation, comprehensive clinical genetic services are offered, including:

- Carrier screening;
- Prenatal screening;
- Newborn screening and diagnosis;
- Presymptomatic screening; and
- Genetic screening.

GETTING GENETIC HELP FOR PSYCHOLOGICAL ISSUES

Psychological screening is only now becoming available for use with adoptions. No real attempt was made in the past to use psychological instruments to help in adoption placement or in understanding problems. Individual parents have probably always sought out psychologists, family counselors and psychiatrists for help, but new instruments, such as the Stevens Adopt-Match Evaluator (SAME), may make it possible for psychological screening to occur prior to adoption.

Contrary to what many adoption workers believe, parents are often relieved to learn that their children's personalities are in large part inherited. In fact, most birth parents have known this all along. From the day a child is born, they see how he differs from other children in the family, and how his traits resemble theirs or their relatives'. Birth parents can often use their own backgrounds and behaviors to guess why their children are acting certain ways. Adoptive parents don't have that kind of intuition, however, and must have genetic information if they are to understand their children in the same way.

If preadoptive testing is not done, a psychological evaluation that includes the Stevens Adopt-Match Evaluator can help the adoptive parents understand the temperament and style of their adopted child. Using that information, it is important for them to learn to accept the inherited personality traits and not demand that the child change.

It is the authors' belief that behavior can change, but personality acceptance is necessary. Inherited traits are neither positive nor negative. It is our experience that the traits themselves are probably neutral, and the environment affects how the traits get acted out, and also how each trait is evaluated. Some families value traits that are not valued by others. Likewise, some cultures value traits that others do not.

Take extroversion, for instance. Depending on how it develops, it may result in pleasant behavior or difficult behavior, and may be valued or looked upon with disdain. Another example is the tendency to be "private." This may be seen by some as a negative trait (shyness) and by others as a positive trait (well-mannered behavior).

Obviously, how personality traits are evaluated by the family will affect the child's self-esteem. Acceptance of the child, either facilitated by preadoptive matching or postadoptive evaluation, should lead to improved communication and a better sense of self-esteem.

CRACKING THE PERSONALITY CODE

Understanding what makes your child tick will help you maximize his/her strengths.

Nature	Nurture	Both
Aggressiveness	Achievement	Artistic sense
Anxiety	Need for intimacy	Athletic prowess
Attention span	Niceness	Leadership
Flexibility		Musical ability
Intelligence		Self-confidence
Resilience		Shyness
Sociability		

Goodness of Fit

Recent studies show that adopted children, who comprise only 2 percent of all children in the United States, account for between 15 and 40 percent of the children being treated in residential or adolescent psychiatric centers.[25] Psychologists are beginning to blame some of these extraordinarily high mental health problems on a poor "family fit."

Researchers Harold Grotevant, Ruth McRoy and Vivian Jenkins suggest that unless developing children are well matched to their physical and social environments, they will suffer painful emotional problems.[26]

No one really knows why adopted children are "at risk" for emotional problems, but data shows that adopted children under age eighteen are referred for psychological treatment two to five times more frequently than nonadopted children. Those figures are for children in America, but researchers in Great Britain, Israel, Poland and Sweden have come to similar conclusions.[27]

One explanation is that most adopted children live in middle-class families, which are more likely to seek help when they perceive a problem. This does not explain, however, why adoptive children might obtain psychological treatment at a higher rate than nonadopted upper-to-middle-class families.

Another recent study found that children referred for psychological treatment are usually in their early or middle-childhood years, when they are dealing with the increased stress of adolescence. It is not unusual for adoptive children to have more severe identity crises as teenagers than their nonadopted peers. In fact, some psychologists refer to these crises as "the adopted child syndrome."

Most adopted children studied by researchers who were referred for residential treatment in their adolescence were adopted as infants by childless couples. Three sets of issues emerge as important in the development of adolescent emotional disturbance:

1. The child's hyperactive behavior;
2. The child's avoidance of contact and cuddling from early infancy on, often called "attachment disorders"; and
3. Perceived incompatibility between the child's personality or temperament and the family's or parents' styles.[28]

The so-called "elbow babies" who push away from care givers in early infancy develop that disorder as a combination of "the child's temperament and the adoptive parents' responsiveness," therapist Michael Orlans writes.

Research shows that children adopted as infants have a better chance of developing a close bond with their new parents unless there is a giant gap in their personality styles. If the children's personality styles are dramatically different than those of members of their families, and if the families don't recognize or can not understand these differences, problems can arise.

Sometimes a child can sense these differences and concludes that he is not the way he is "supposed to be." This may prohibit a close bond with the parents and lead to low self-esteem or rebellious behavior. Some children may try to hide personality traits considered unacceptable by adoptive parents. In the worst cases, matching problems can lead to adoption failure.

A landmark study by Stella Chess and her husband, Alexander Thomas, both M.D.s and professors of psychiatry at New York University, offers proof for the theory that children prosper when matched with families that value their temperaments. The couple followed 133 children from infancy to adulthood and found two main forces at work in shaping the children's personalities: a youngster's temperament and how the parents responded to that temperament.

Drs. Chess and Thomas found that children are, in part, products of their own personalities and what they call "family fit." When they use this term, they are really talking about how the match between parents and children is played out, or how well they understand each other. Their study subjects were not adopted, but their findings apply to the adopted child as well.

"The fit is right when a child learns to feel good about himself and can function well in the world," explains Dr. Chess.[29] As described by the couple, "family fit" doesn't mean that parents and children always feel in tune with each other or that everyone in the family has the same personality. Rather, it means that everyone is valued for who he or she is. With a good "family fit" it is possible for adopted children and their families to function as one, to feel in tune.

PERCEIVED INCOMPATIBILITY

One adoptive father studied by Grotevant described the "fit" problems he had with an adoptive son. "My wife and I come from 'walk-the-straight-and-narrow-path' kinds of backgrounds," he said. "Our tolerance range is pretty narrow!"[30]

Their son's difficult behavior fell outside that range, and it nearly tore the family apart. The man admits that a more tolerant family might have been better for the child, and counsels other prospective families to pay attention to personality traits that may be "totally incongruent" with their own.

"Don't feel weird about taking [an adopted child] back and trying somebody else," he says. "The blackest part of my whole life is having that kid and everything that it's done to our family."

Although his advice may sound harsh, this father speaks for other adoptive parents driven to distraction by personality mismatches. One mother cited in Grotevant's study described herself as "sedentary" and her child as "hyperactive." Another couple called themselves "industrious and affectionate," while their adopted son was "lazy and distant." Yet another couple said they were introverted, while their daughter was outgoing. The ability of these parents to acknowledge their children's heredity and go forward is crucial if the adoption is to succeed.

"WE GOT THE WRONG CHILD"

In the case of one adopted child having problems, we found a father who is logical and values cause-and-effect thinking. His adopted son is very impulsive, artistic and imaginative, with little ability to delay gratification. When the child gets in trouble, the father has no way of understanding it. He has always believed that hard work and careful teaching will correct his son's problems.

The man may or may not be right. He will never be able to "correct his son's personality," no matter how hard he tries, but he may be able to understand it. As long as he expects the boy to be like him, the father will never understand and may never be able to help the child.

His experience is not unique. Grotevant found that many adoptive families "noted discrepancies between their children's personalities and what was acceptable within the context of their family." Once they recognized those discrepancies, "a self-protective ... process typically began," Grotevant writes. "Parents told themselves, 'It's not our fault. It must be because he is adopted.' Abdication of ownership of the problem by the parents often signaled an early stage in the emotional distancing of the adoptive parents from their child."[31]

All but one of eight adoptive families studied by Grotevant had another child, either adopted or biological. The parents' perception of the newly adopted child as "somehow different" reflected their opinion that they had gotten a bad kid. Some even believed the agency had gotten the wrong child for them. This perceived difference can set the stage for dissatisfaction in the parent-child relationship, setting up a self-fulfilling prophecy. Specialists say that without help in reframing the family's attitudes, it is not unusual for these perceptions to turn into strongly entrenched convictions that the adopted child does not belong in the family.

That may be why many social workers in the adoption field avoid sharing their children's hereditary histories with prospective parents. A group of California social workers interviewed by Jerome Kagan and Nancy Snidman for *American Psychologist* magazine, the journal of the American Psychological Association, said that viewing a child's problems as a result of heredity brings up new problems they are trying to avoid.

They said they were afraid adoptive families would reject children thought to have hereditary problems, and feared that low expectations would be self-fulfilling. If a family is told their child may be mentally challenged, for example, they might treat that child as if she was learning-impaired, and she might learn to act that way.

"It is easier to be persuaded that [a person can more effectively] monitor moods and behaviors if they were learned than if they were influenced ... by the person's inherent biology," write Kagan and Snidman in *American Psychologist*.[32] Yet this way of thinking is "neither logical nor empirically proven," they add.

The social workers they interviewed said they thought adoptive parents would start looking for problems if hereditary information were given a larger role, blaming behaviors they do not (or can not) understand on the "child's background" rather than examining their own parenting techniques and accepting responsibility for their role in creating or solving the problem.

Ignoring a child's heredity can also bring problems, Grotevant writes. His research found that adoptive parents who either diminish or accentuate the importance of an adopted child's heredity to an extreme degree create an incompatibility with the child.[33]

CREATING A FAMILY THROUGH MATCHING

The best solution is to test all prospective parents and adoptable children before the adoption to allow for the closest match possible. Tools such as the Stevens Adopt-Match Evaluator (SAME) make it possible to determine important aspects of temperament ahead of time. The goal is to re-create the ease with which birth parents can raise their children by carefully matching the personality styles of adoptive children and parents. With the right "family fit," it is possible even for children born with predispositions for problems to become more productive, contributing adults.

It is also important that adoption workers watch for the following problems, which can create a feeling of "wrong child/wrong family":

- Physical dissimilarities;
- Personality dissimilarities;
- Style dissimilarities; or
- Psychological problems in the child.

If families haven't been carefully matched, however, it is important to help parents understand the ways in which their children are different from them and to learn to respect those differences. The input of a psychologist or counselor may be necessary.

AT-RISK CHILDREN

It becomes more difficult when we look at a child's potential predisposition to mental illness. Experts in the field believe parents who are warned of potential genetic problems and given good training, information and follow-up will be able to teach, train and help their adopted child.

Understanding these children is sometimes difficult, however. A child with emotional or behavioral problems may be unlikable and may try the patience of his adoptive parents. The authors can not emphasize enough that parents taking on special-needs children need extensive pre- and postadoption placement counseling to be prepared for any problems that will arise, whether they are personality differences or predispositions.

Says adoption expert Daniel T. Adams of the Hand-in-Hand International Adoption Agency, "We want these parents to be prepared for what they will face. Parents need to know that things will not always go smoothly. They need to know that everything will not be just fine once they get the child home."[34]

Conclusions

What better way to maximize the successful placement of an older, waiting child than by testing for temperament and matching families and children with similar qualities? Many children come with "excess baggage" due to medical problems, psychological problems caused by early abuse or fragile genetics. Being placed with incompatible parents who are unable to understand them can compound their problems.

To dispel the prevalent myth that love and a positive environment will solve all problems, adoption professionals must be attuned to the importance of genetic characteristics and share them with prospective parents. Parents must also be candid about the kinds of personality traits they are prepared to deal with.

Problems with temperament mismatches do not have to occur. Using new testing tools such as the SAME, it is now easier to match a child with a family in which she can feel secure and loved and grow into a productive adult, a family in which the child "fits."

The authors believe that any child can learn anything, given appropriate intelligence, but first we must start with where the child is. If we begin by understanding and respecting who the child is, we will have a better chance of teaching what we want him to learn. By respecting the child's temperament, we help ourselves to a better outcome.

For example, if we have a child who shies away from new experiences and we try to force him into new situations, we may be breaking a bond of communication and trust by not empathizing with the child's view of the world. On the other hand, if we get into the child's view of the world, we may be able, from that perspective, to help the child change in a way that we can accept.

The authors say that, with the right education and the right family fit, children's environments can help them heal. Adoptive parents can help these at-risk children become productive adults. Taking nature into account, nurture can help. But it requires the right match.

Where temperament matching has been taken into account, bonding will likely proceed normally. Young children respond to their environment by trying to adapt to it, by learning to please adults. This is much more possible when they are more similar to the adults they are trying to please.

At the same time, we need to remember that these children are on a time clock. If we had all the time and resources we need, it would be possible to make exact matches, including such things as ethnic background, physical appearance and personality. In the process of waiting, however, we may be losing the chance for a real bond.

---

[1] D'Antonio, *Child* magazine, 1990, p. 62.

[2] Ibid., p. 63.

[3] Ibid.

[4] Thomas J. Bouchard, et al., *Science* magazine, 250, p. 223–28.

[5] Ibid.

[6] Ibid.

[7] Adam Matheny, *APA Monitor*, 22, no. 1 (January 1991).

[8] Robert Plomin, "Environment and Genes: Determinants of Behavior," *American Psychologist*, (February 1989): pp. 105–8.

[9] Ibid.

[10] *CareNetwork* (March/April 1989): pp. 18–19.

[11] Ibid.

[12] Robert Plomin, personal correspondence, December 1990.

[13] Plomin, "Environment and Genes," p. 107.

[14] "Joan Steel," personal interview, Los Angeles, California, August 1991.

[15] Plomin, "Environment and Genes," p. 108.

[16] "Swedish Adoption Study," *Caring*, vol. 11, no. 2 (Spring 1986).

[17] *CareNetwork*, p. 17.

[18] "Swedish Adoption Study," *Caring*.

[19] Ibid., p. 33.

[20] Ibid.

[21] *Caring* (Fall 1990).

[22] Foster Cline, M.D., personal interview, Evergreen, Colorado, January 1991.

[23] Julia B. Rauch and Nancy Rike, *Adoption Worker's Guide to Genetic Services*.

[24] Ibid.

[25] Michael Orlans, *Attachments* (Spring 1993).

[26] Harold Grotevant, Ruth McRoy and Vivian Jenkins, "Emotionally Disturbed, Adopted Adolescents: Early Patterns of Family Adaptation," *Family Process, Inc.*, (1988): pp. 439–57.

[27] Orlans, *Attachments*.

[28] Ibid.

[29] Stella Chess, M.D. and Alexander Thomas, M.D., *Family Circle* (February 1991): pp. 45–46.

[30] Grotevant, et al., "Emotionally Disturbed, Adopted Adolescents," p. 440.

[31] Ibid., p. 453.

[32] Jerome Kagan and Nancy Snidman, *American Psychologist*, vol. 46, no. 8, August, 1991, p. 862.

[33] Grotevant, et al., "Emotionally Disturbed, Adopted Adolescents," pp. 439–57.

[34] Daniel T. Adams, personal interview, Colorado Springs, Colorado, March 25, 1991.

CHAPTER TEN

THE MULTICULTURAL DEBATE

Lucky that man
Whose children make his happiness in life
And not his grief,
the anguished disappointment of his hopes
Euripides,
Orestes

Race is one biological trait that can not be ignored. For decades, child welfare workers have debated the pros and cons of matching Anglo parents with children of color, without reaching a concensus. Should race be the single most determining factor in a child's placement, or are other considerations more important? Several adoptive families and adopted children have strong feelings about their experiences.

A Multicultural Adoption Story

Trisha Flynn-Cheroutes and her husband, Michael Cheroutes, adopted Trisha Francesca, whom they call Checka, from Denver County Social Services when she was seven months old. That was during the height of the 1970s adoption era.

The couple already had a son and wanted a daughter, so bira-cial Checka joined their family. She was the second child born to a fifteen-year-old Hispanic mother and a sixteen- or seventeen-year-old African-American father. That couple kept their first child, a boy, but put Checka up for adoption.

The Cheroutes' son was about the same age, "so they grew up almost like twins," Trisha remembers. "Everything was done in pairs. We just didn't think about the adoption part too much." Even so, Checka always felt "different."[1]

"No one looked like her," Trisha says, but her mixed racial background thrust her into the position of celebrity among '70s Anglo liberals. "She got preferential treatment from the adults, and she was used to it. She was bright, precocious, mouthy and tied into adults, but with other children she was bossy and mean.

"Teachers adored her and made her feel special, which the other kids didn't like at all," her mother says. "I spent a lot of time at school, telling them to treat her like the other kids. But it didn't work very well." The upshot was that Checka became the teacher's pet and did very well academically. "This may have had to do with me," Trisha sighs. "I had her reading novels in elementary school."

Even at age two, however, Checka showed signs of emotional problems. She was extremely abusive to animals, "deliberately doing things like pulling on them or gouging at their eyes," Trisha says. "This was something I couldn't accept. Finally, when she realized they had feelings and could be hurt, she learned not to do that."

Trisha later understood where the problems came from. As an infant, Checka had been in a foster home with four children under five years old. "This meant she got zip," her mother says. "She had gotten used to a propped bottle and would move her head from side to side and scream for a bottle [when we first got her]. But she was cuddly and had good eye contact. We could tell she was extremely bright ... and we just knew she was the one for us."

Even though Checka had been deprived, she caught up "in no time," Trisha says. "Once the opportunities were offered, she just took off. She had just had no ... opportunities."

Dealing with the racial problems wasn't as easy. Trisha still feels it is best to place children with parents of the same race when adopting, "but common sense tells you there aren't enough parents for some of these children," she says. "It's certainly better to have a family than not."

Trisha tried to help Checka learn about her heritage, making sure to send her to racially integrated schools (her first preschool had a black teacher), living in integrated neighborhoods and teaching her what they could about her culture.

"One thing that helped is that about 20 percent of our friends are black," Trisha adds, "although we did not change our lifestyles. We didn't make an effort to give her just black dolls. When one child got something, they all did, but we did have a year when everyone got little black dolls."

Trisha says Checka, now twenty-one, has turned out to be very much like them. "My child didn't have the perfect childhood, but she is loved and she is very much like us. There are enormous differences and enormous similarities." As far as racial identity, Trisha says she thinks Checka feels black, even though she is also half Hispanic. Surprisingly, the child's first exposure to prejudice was from black high-school friends, who told her she could no longer have white friends.

During those high-school years, Checka's life was so turbulent "I wish she had taken a slow boat to China, and I would have paid the passage," Trisha says. The problems started when she was enrolled in a Catholic high school.

"You're talking about a middle-class white momma who is protective," she explains, "so we sent her to a Catholic boarding school like I had been to. It was a mistake." Checka failed miserably at the parochial school and finally pushed so hard that she was expelled.

"She was always testing to see how much others could take. When she physically 'acted out' she beat the hell out of another kid. She got into every kind of trouble she could, short of being expelled, and finally she was [even expelled]."

Much therapy later, Checka finished her high-school requirements in one semester at the private, nonprofit Accelerated School in Denver. She is now looking into career options and talks about finding her birth parents. Trisha is hopeful about Checka's future, but says she still isn't sure if Anglo parents should adopt children of color.

Checka's story brings up a number of issues about interracial adoption that are still being debated today, including:

- What barriers are there to same-race adoption?
- What barriers are there to mixed-race adoption?
- Can mixed-race families work?
- Does the primarily Anglo adoptive system serve children of color adequately?
- Why do children of color comprise over half of the children waiting for homes?
- How do we increase families of color in the adoption arena?

American Minority Children Are Waiting

The adoption of children of color by Anglo parents is one of the most controversial issues in adoption today. Does interracial adoption deprive children of their culture or result in low self-esteem, and should it be allowed to continue?

In reality, few Anglo parents are allowed to adopt children of another race. Most states require adoptive parents and children to be matched for ethnic and racial backgrounds, even though the reality is that 51 percent of the thirty-four thousand children free for adoption in the early '90s were children of color, about 80 percent of whom had special needs. Many had spent years waiting for ethnically matched parents.

One reason may be that parents of color are in short supply because they hit roadblocks when trying to adopt. Studies show that when barriers are removed, families of color readily welcome children into their homes.

RACE BARRIERS REMAIN

In one recent study conducted by the North American Council on Adoptable Children (NACAC), eighty-seven private and public child-placing agencies in twenty-five states were surveyed about barriers that discourage families of color from adopting.[2] The agencies had placed 13,208 children in 1991, and although nearly half were children of color, 83 percent of the respondents said they were aware of organizational and institutional barriers that tended to discourage families of color.

Agencies who specialized in placement of minority children had the best results—they found same-race homes for 95 percent of the children—but other private agencies were able to place only 51 percent of their black and Hispanic children in same-race homes. Poor record keeping at the public level made it hard to calculate the results of public agencies.

Researchers also found that children of color placed through public and specialized agencies are often older or have special needs, yet are still placed with same-race families at higher rates than healthy infants placed by traditional agencies.[3]

Only a few cross-cultural and cross-ethnic adoptions are allowed, but those that do occur bring with them a slew of unique problems that must be overcome.

WHAT THE STUDIES SAY

How well do interracially adopted children really do? Just fine, many researchers say. Some research data indicates clearly that children fare well with adoptive parents of another race. One study found these children to have as much sense of security as children in same-race adoptions. Another study found "no major differences in [interracial adoptees'] levels of self-esteem, although the way that they perceived their racial identities did differ slightly."

Still, a vocal group of black social workers say more should be done to promote adoption within the minority community, and housing and income barriers that exclude minority families should be removed from adoption requirements. Dr. Morris Jeff, president of the National Black Social Workers Association, stated that "we strongly believe blacks should adopt black children and, if provided an opportunity to do so, will. Our position is that the African-American family should be maintained and its integrity preserved."[4] He and other critics of interracial adoption say the practice causes "severe psychological problems during adolescence and adulthood."

The first step is revising the fee schedule. Dixie van de Flier Davis, director of the Rocky Mountain Adoption Exchange, says minority families that would be good for these children are not families that can afford to pay, or believe in the ethics of paying, for the service of adoption. "Minority families find that to be really offensive," she says. "It's like buying a child, and [to them] it makes no sense."

To prove her point, Davis says: "We go on television saying, 'We need a family, a black family, for this beautiful little four-month-old.' Then [couples] call and find out there is a $5,000 fee attached."[5] Most don't follow through.

BARRIERS TO PLACEMENTS

- *Institutional/Systemic Racism.* With just about all guidelines impacting standard agency adoption developed from white middle-class perspectives.
- *A Lack of People of Color in Management.* The agency board of directors and heads remain mostly white.
- *Fees.* Most of the agencies said adoption fees are a barrier to minority families wishing to adopt. (It is not necessarily that they do not have money, but that they are morally opposed to "paying" for a child.)
- *"Adoption as Business" Mentality/Reality.* Because of their dependence on fees for income, many agencies are forced to place transracially to ensure survival.
- *Communities of Color Historical Tendencies Toward "Informal" Adoption.* Adopters of color question the relevance of formalized adoption procedures, believing them unnecessary.
- *Negative Perceptions of Agencies and Their Practices.* Families of color traditionally have negative perceptions of public and private agencies and their motives.
- *Lack of Minority Staff.* More minority workers are needed in the "trenches" to build trust among families of color.
- *Inflexible Standards.* Insistence upon a rigid, young, two-parent, materially possessed family eliminates many people of color.
- *General Lack of Recruitment and Poor Recruitment Techniques.* Agencies find themselves unable to set aside financial and human resources for effective recruitment.
- *Word Not Out.* Communities of color are not aware of the large need for their services.

The primary lesson to be learned from these statistics is that agencies committed to same-race placements must work harder, especially in the areas of recruitment and flexibility. They must try to screen families *into* the system and not *out* of it. Staff must be available at times convenient for prospective parents, and the staff itself needs to be more culturally diversified.

In reality, closely matched ethnic backgrounds may not be all children need from their adoptive families. Even in same-race families, adoptive children and their adoptive parents may not be compatible; their personalities may not mesh.

THE WRONG FAMILY

At six weeks old, tiny Michelle was taken in by her great aunt and uncle in Wichita Falls, Texas, because her birth mother could not take care of her. Six months later, her relatives adopted her and re-named her Gloria, "a more Hispanic name."

Now twenty-one, Gloria says the family match was painfully wrong, even though she is half Hispanic and half Caucasian. She never felt like she fit into the old-style Mexican household.

"My adopted parents are still living in the 1940s," Gloria says. "They are functionally illiterate, speaking only Spanish as a first language. My adopted father doesn't speak much English, and he doesn't read or write it at all. My mother can read my letters, but I have to use small words. If I use big words she gets mad.[6]

"I was like a sore thumb in the family," Gloria remembers. "I didn't fit in. I went to school and did well [while most of her adopted siblings dropped out]." And although Spanish was the family's first language, Gloria always thought in English.

She was also physically different than the others in her family. They are short and obese with very black hair. She is tall and thin with blond hair and fair skin. "If you looked at a family picture, your reaction would be, 'Where on earth did they get her?'" The differences were not lost on family members. One brother gave her the nickname "Gueda," which means "Whitey."

"Oh, it was meant as cute, not mean," she explains, "but I've always been different in one way or another. I'm just more English, which was odd in school. I always had to tell people I was Spanish, and when they didn't get it, I'd say, 'Hey, I'm Gloria *Garcia,* doesn't that say anything to you?'"

The woman also regrets the age difference between her adoptive mother (sixty-nine) and her birth mother (forty-three). "My adoptive mother already had three girls and two sons when I was adopted, and the youngest was eleven or twelve," she says. "All my siblings are much older than me."

Gloria is an example of something Colorado therapist Connell Watkins feels strongly about. "Race doesn't have anything to do with [compatibility]!" she says.[7] One of her pet peeves is caseworkers who let children wait in foster homes until parents of the same race come along to adopt them.

NOT A BLACK-AND-WHITE ISSUE

The issue has never been black and white, but Watkins is just one of many therapists who believe children may be better nourished by families of similiar personality styles or temperament than by families that are only ethnically similar.

Fos/Adopt mother Debbe Magnusen has had children from all different backgrounds—a "rainbow of color," as she describes them. Yet she hasn't been able to adopt a black infant because of roadblocks set up to discourage multiracial adoptions.

She is angry at the "backward" thinking that refuses to place these needy minority children in white or mixed-race households. "The issue should be bonding, not color," she says. "How can we deny these babies of a different color or nationality a home? In my opinion, that is reverse discrimination."[8]

Conclusions

Children need families for a lifetime, and they need them from the moment they are born. Yet as the debate about interracial adoption continues, the need for it has never been higher. Unless more enthusiasm can be mustered for interracial adoptions, or unless other solutions can be found, thousands of eager parents and minority babies will be the victims. Both are being discriminated against.

In the best of worlds, children should be placed in families of like race, and we can do much to make that easier. We can change the guidelines for adoptive parents and make the fee schedule more flexible, but race must still be considered just one standard for matching. We do not have the best of worlds today, and we must make do with what we have. The authors believe that children can find homes in which they will have a "family fit," whether they match in color or not.

The truth is that a young life is a terrible thing to waste, and children of color left in limbo while waiting for same-race parents are doomed to a life without roots. All children deserve a chance for love and a home, and we need to pay attention to all aspects of their needs.

---

[1] Trisha Flynn-Cheroutes, personal interview, Denver, Colorado, Summer 1991.

[2] Tom Gilles and Joe Kroll, North American Council on Adoptable Children, Executive Director, *Barriers to Same-Race Placement,* 1991.

[3] Tom Gilles and Joe Kroll, North American Council on Adoptable Children, *Adoptalk* (Spring 1991): pp. 1-3.

[4] W. Leavy, "Should Whites Adopt Black Children?" *Ebony* magazine, p. 178.

[5] Dixie van de Flier Davis, personal interview, Denver, Colorado, January 1991.

[6] Gloria Garcia, personal interview, Houston, Texas, 1990.

[7] Connell Watkins, personal interview, Evergreen, Colorado, Spring 1993.

[8] Debbe Magnusen, personal interview, August 1992.

CHAPTER ELEVEN

THE ADOPTION TRIAD: LOSS AND HEALING

How sharper than a serpent's tooth it is
To have a thankless child.
                                Shakespeare,
                                King Lear

Adoption is never over for any of the parties involved. It makes a lifelong impact on birth parents, adoptive parents and adoptees alike, characterized by feelings of grief and loss that are ever-present, even if they sometimes are vague. Birth parents grieve for the child they gave away; the child grieves for parents and family history he or she will never know. Adoptive parents grieve for the biological child they will never know, and for the pain they can not seem to help their adopted children overcome.

Adoptees have compared themselves to amputees, struggling to understand how and why they lost their limbs, always hoping to heal from the ordeal and feeling guilty that they haven't. Some feel inadequate because they just don't seem to fit in their adoptive families. Others are consumed with anger at parents who threw them away like yesterday's news.

"Russ" has spent his life feeling inadequate and trying to figure out why.

Never Really Fitting In

Russ used to feel proud and lucky when he reflected on being adopted. He told Dr. JoEllen Stevens in therapy sessions that he felt lucky to be alive and not with his birth mother. Actually, all he knew about his birth mother was what his adoptive mother told him—that she probably was on welfare, had several other kids who were abused and neglected and one child who had died from "being left too long on one side so his brain was flattened," he was told. [1]

When Russ was born in a Los Angeles County hospital thirty-four years ago, his adoptive parents were waiting for him. He had some problems immediately following birth, but no one really knew what kind. He says the Privacy Act prevented his parents from learning what happened in his first two hours of life, but after that time he was released to them.

Russ isn't really sure why his parents adopted him. "They wanted to have children," he explains, "but maybe they didn't have time." They adopted four before giving birth to two. Half joking, Russ says they wanted "farm labor."

Russ grew up believing that he was special because he was chosen. That made him feel even worse when he reflected on his problems. He felt completely responsible for being a failure.

He was two when he realized that there were problems. "I didn't pick up things easily, like games, sports," Russ says. "It took longer no matter how hard I tried. Then my anxiety and anger came out. I had a feeling I didn't fit in in general, in church, at camp, farming, at school. I was in special ed. I was such a brat ... really uncontrollable."

At age five or six, Russ concluded that he was to blame for his problems. "My mom would say, 'He is a good baby when he's asleep.' I was a troubled kid." He was also uncoordinated, off kilter all the time. At age five he fell off a haystack and hit his head on a steel truck bed. Now he has bad hearing that is degenerative.

When Russ was diagnosed as manic-depressive at age twenty-four, he remembers feeling relieved. He thought that since he finally knew what was wrong with him, everything would be okay.

"It's been ten years since then, and I haven't been able to fix it," Russ says. "I haven't been able to work since I was hospitalized two and a half years ago. Even before that I could only keep a job for three to six months. I would do real good for a short while, then I would make some kind of mistake, and I couldn't deal with it. I would walk off the job. I felt worthless.

"I was never good enough for my dad. He worked ten to fourteen hours a day and expected me to also. When I was five, I worked four hours a day. At age ten, I worked eight hours a day in the summer. At eighteen it was ten to fourteen hours a day, but it still wasn't good enough."

Even today Russ falls into a childlike state when he makes a mistake, even if it's a minor one. In this childlike state he becomes helpless, hopeless and worthless. Worst of all, he can not help himself. He reverts to old behaviors, including temper tantrums, rage and "acting out."

"I guess I just gave up. I kept hoping someone would help me, find the right medication, or whatever, but I just gave up. My rage was out of control at myself," Russ admits, "and I took it out on everyone."

Russ still loves his parents, but he is angry at them. It was only after he began to accept the anger that he began to forgive himself and them. "I have learned to understand that it wasn't my fault," he says. "They did the best they could, but they didn't know how to parent me. I was just a kid, and I couldn't do it myself. I'm just now learning how to parent myself."

Russ' disability makes him feel very low and effeminate. Because his family valued work above everything else, and he isn't very good at working, he has had trouble learning to value himself.

"Men are supposed to work and support their families," he explains. "I left wives the same way I left jobs, because I wasn't good enough."

Russ is afraid to feel hopeful about his future. He's still scared about working and quitting and feeling worthless all over again. "But this is my plan," he says. "I plan to be back at work, maybe part time, by the end of six months.

"Sometimes I still feel very weak. I get down on myself because I can't stop smoking even though it's now causing me health problems. I can't stop eating even though I've gained all this weight. But I have learned more about myself and am trying to be more accepting. I just can't be who they wanted me to be."

There are many like Russ. Not all are disabled or have emotional problems, but many adoptees over the years have felt inadequate because they didn't fit in. They had no way of knowing that they were born different, or that it is okay to be different. They just felt wrong.

In the past, before adoption workers knew anything about personality matching, many such mistakes were made. Even without mismatches between child and parent, however, adoptees often feel grief and loss without knowing why. There is something lost in adoption, even as there is something gained. And many times adoptive parents are so busy with their own problems they fail to—or don't want to—recognize their child's sense of loss.

One adoptive mother let her daughter know just how she felt when the sixteen-year-old wondered aloud what her birth mother was like. The woman said she let her know "in no uncertain terms" that she was her mother—her only mother. The girl never asked again.

Most adoptive children experience loss—the loss of the relationship that might have been, the loss of being told "I was just like you as a child"—even if they don't realize what is lost. They may feel "wrong" or "inadequate" without knowing why.

"Richard" is another grown man who never really developed a close relationship with his adoptive parents. Adopted at birth, Richard spent twenty-five years feeling like he didn't fit into the family. At the same time, he says he has "a bond" with the birth mother he has never met, although he has been afraid to track her down.

"On my birthday, I spend the whole day thinking about her," he says, "and I know she's thinking about me, too." Only after extensive therapy for emotional problems—including depression and difficulty with relationships with women—did Richard decide it was time to begin searching for the mother he never knew. He joined thousands of other adult adoptees searching for their roots.[2]

Past generations believed it was best not to tell children they were adopted. They thought the best way to save children from the grief of losing their family was to protect them from the truth: If they didn't know, they wouldn't hurt. Insecure adoptive parents, overwhelmed with their own feelings about miscarriages and their inability to get pregnant, usually were more than happy to go along with the deception.

Their mistake was ignoring genetics. No one can erase a child's genes—the color of his eyes, the way she walks, her tendency toward impulsive behavior, his inclination to be quiet. We are learning that children can not be taken from one "batch" and put with another without explanation. We need to understand more about the nature of the batch so that the child's new environment makes sense in relation to who he is.

WALT CONLEY

Walter Conley was such a child. As a small, black child, he knew something was wrong, just felt it, even before any of his problems appeared.

He grew up in Scottsbluff, Nebraska, the only child of Emma and Wallace Conley. As he entered elementary school, other children began to taunt him. They said, "I know something about you, and if I told you it would make you cry."

The teasing went on and on, Conley remembers vividly, "but I couldn't figure out what it might be. One time I was really scared. I thought I might be dying, or my parents might be real sick, but the kids wouldn't tell me. I think their parents had said never to tell me, or else!"

It was an adult woman who finally spilled the beans, blurting out the truth without realizing she had just delivered a direct hit on Walter's sense of well-being. It happened one night when Conley and his mother had gone to a movie and were waiting outside the theater for his father to pick them up.

"A white lady came over and said, 'Oh, Edna, I haven't seen you for such a long time.' I was just standing there, you know ... when she turned to her friend to introduce us," Conley says. "She said, 'This is my friend Edna, you've heard me talk about her so much and this is her little adopted boy ... uh? ... '

"I remember my mother said softly, 'Walter,' and that was the end of it. I felt like I was going to explode, like a bomb had gone off. It had never occurred to me that I might be adopted. You know what

I did at that moment? I pretended I didn't hear it right. She couldn't mean *me*."

The next morning, his parents told him the truth. He remembers sitting on his mother's knees, feeling awkward to be sitting there at age eight or nine, and starting to cry. Instead of comforting him, his father got angry.

"'What are you crying for?' my father said. 'We've given you a wonderful home and life. We've loved you like our own.' And then he hit me, can you imagine? My relationship with my family was never the same from that moment on," Conley says. "It all changed. I became sort of a bad kid."

Still, when his father died when Walter was thirteen, the young man took it very hard. They had just begun to get close again. His mother couldn't stand to stay in the town anymore, so they made a series of moves. Conley remembers it as "a hard time."

Now a professional singer and entertainer, Conley says he has always been awkward about starting new experiences, like going on the road, going to new places. "I'm always sort of apprehensive," he says. "I think it comes from that insecurity as a child."[3]

Conley's adoption in the 1930s was typical for the day. Children simply weren't told the truth unless someone else exposed it. He eventually was told that his parents found out from a friend about this "baby that needed to be adopted, in Denver." They drove the 180 miles and picked him up at the Colorado Home for Dependent Children. He was the youngest of seven siblings and had medical problems, which is "probably why I was given up," he guesses. "[My birth family] couldn't afford one more, especially one that was sick."

He also knows his original name was Billie Harris, which would make it very hard to track down his birth family. "It couldn't be worse if my name was Smith," he says. "Imagine how many Harris's there are out there."

Conley has not tried to find them, explaining that he didn't want to intrude on another family, "you know, a stranger," but he has diabetes and is curious about his genetic background. "Some of my brothers or sisters are probably still living," he says. "I might try to find them one of these days."

The Adoptee as Amputee?

Joan Keres was adopted as a toddler. One of her biggest sorrows is losing her birth heritage and family history.

She is Hispanic, but was adopted into an immigrant Czechoslovakian family. Although she has done the best she can in researching her background and trying to live her birth heritage, she feels she can never recapture the rich family stories and history she lost at birth.

Keres still awakes in the middle of the night, shaking from the memory of a recurring nightmare. In the dream, her chest is ripped off from her neck to her naval. She interprets the dream as a reminder that she was torn from her mother's arms as a small child. It brings her to tears, as does talking about her adoption.

"You don't think," she gasps, desperately, "you don't think I will have this with me forever? That I'll never get over it? I've tried everything, psychotherapy, prayer, body work, you name it, but I can not forget."[4]

Keres also spent years searching for her birth parents, only to find a woman who is mentally ill. "I'm glad I did, but my mother is not really of this earth," she says. "She has never recovered from losing her children—my brother and me. She is literally out of her mind."

Is Keres "an amputee," as author Linda Brown describes it in her book, *Birthbound*? Or is she just another aching adoptee who fears she may never be able to reestablish her relationship with an absent (in her case, mentally ill) mother?

A poet and storyteller, Keres has written about her loss:

Soy Desaparacido

> There are other ways to disappear
> Besides Los Hombres del Muerte
> (the death squads)
> Now that I see my aging immediately
> better than in a mirror
> or from any little incident with an *amorato*,
> a lover ...
> At this age, the double shovel of 44,

I am older probably than
my great, great, great, great, great, grandmother
ever lived to be, what with puerperal fever and all.
I wonder did she hang poems on the rocks
along with the white shirts she washed in the river?
Did she iron the lines down as she ground the *masa* ...
What better way to get the rhythm of a poem
than rolling *maize* into paste?
How can these five, or these thousands of generations
of my kinswomen disappear like *polvo*, like dust
in the adoption transaction.
Why can't I just peel down my bloodlines
like wallpaper and find
the women of my dreamtime, my own *cantadora* line.
The only place I see them
These women poets who were rinsed away by
the signature on legal paper,
the only time I see them is in the dreams,
when we write together,
when we sing, when we tell the old stories.
I know there were women in my bloodline
who were like me, and though they couldn't write
or read, I know they could sing.
Yes, to begin anything at all,
I must first bow to the generations
of my female bloodline
wiped out
with the stroke
of a pen.

Joan Keres, © 1990

The Healing Process

Reestablishing relationships can be an important part of the healing process for adults adopted as children. The process is filled with fear of the unknown, but adoptees who have found their birth parents say it has one guaranteed benefit—it brings the uncertainty to an end and replaces it with reality. Sometimes the reality is harsh and sometimes sweet, but it is always real. As such, it can destroy childhood fantasies of what might have been.

Some adult adoptees have found reality difficult to live with. It is disheartening to search for a birth parent, only to find out that she is dead. If that's the case, at least it is possible to mourn the loss and go forward without uncertainty. Acceptance of reality is just that—allowing whatever is to be.

There are as many different stories as there are adult adoptees who search for and find a parent. Many of them are wonderful stories, a few of them are sad and some bring up issues that are difficult to resolve. Rebecca's is one.

At nineteen, Rebecca found out that her birth father had died four months earlier of alcoholism. She was still in shock from the discovery when she got a call from an aunt she didn't know about. The woman, her father's sister, was gracious and loving and wanted to meet her.

Rebecca did go to meet her aunt, and in doing so she discovered a large family of cousins, aunts and uncles willing to talk with her about her father. She described it as the "opening up of a whole new world," a world of people who loved her that she never dreamed could exist.

Adoption always involves loss, but sometimes it also involves rediscovery. If adopted children are brought up to understand the loss, however, they may not suffer another devastating loss—the loss of faith and trust that Walter Conley experienced. Even children raised by family members such as grandmothers or stepparents feel deceived when they aren't told the truth.

Such was the case of Heather, the adopted stepdaughter of author Carole McKelvey. Now a thirty-five-year-old single parent of two, Heather suffers the consequences of being shielded from the truth about her heritage. She is the adopted child of McKelvey's husband, George. When the child was small, her mother, Penny, married George and told Heather he was her birth father rather than her adopted father.

In the early '60s, Heather remembers living in Chicago with her parents and sister, Erin, not far from George's parents. "We visited them often and I grew to love them dearly," she says. "My life was filled with security and certainty of what was going to happen from day to day. My parents became folk singers and sang in night clubs, which was very exciting for me. Erin and I were extremely close. I was seven."[5]

Her happiness was shattered later that year when George took the girls into the car and told them he was leaving home. "He started to explain that he couldn't live with us and Mom anymore," Heather remembers. "He said it was just for awhile, and that he would come back in a few months. Mom and he were not getting along and had to be apart for a time." Soon after, Erin was sent to live with an aunt, and Heather moved in with her grandparents while their parents pursued solo careers.

"The feelings of insecurity and unhappiness began to set in as I waited for my father to come back," Heather says. "I believed him when he said he would. He visited me a few times, but I began to wonder if he loved me."

When she was nine, Heather joined her mother and sister in an apartment outside of Chicago. Her mother was still singing and struggling to make ends meet. She missed George, who visited infrequently, but she saw her grandparents often.

"I trusted them, loved them and believed everything they told me," she said. Eventually, the family moved in with another family of three, a woman and her two daughters. When Heather was twelve, her mother went to California to promote her singing career and left the girls with the other woman.

"Our mother never came back," Heather says. "I was very scared. It was just like what my father had done. Did anyone love me enough to stick around?"

A year later George did come back to claim the girls, something Heather describes as "a dream come true," but they didn't live happily ever after. He brought a new wife, Carole McKelvey, and "he was *unprepared* for us," Heather says. "I remember a lot of yelling and putting down of teenagers. I felt unwanted, and went to San Francisco to live with mother. Erin stayed with our dad for six months longer, and then joined us in San Francisco."

Heather's insecurities began to subside until her grandmother said something that brought things to a head. "I went to visit my grandparents, and I was sitting at the kitchen table," she says. "My grand-mother was brushing my hair when, seemingly out of nowhere, she told me, 'Even though we're not blood-related, I love you just the same as if I was your real grandmother.' At first I didn't understand what she meant. After a couple of very long minutes, I started to cry as it began to sink in. I was shaking—felt faint—as she began to explain to me that her son married my mother when I was six months old.

"Like a flash flood, it finally made sense to me, why my father never came back, why he always favored my sister, ... why I didn't look like anyone in the family. I felt like I was being killed."

When they found out what she had done, both parents were very angry at Heather's grandmother. "Apparently my adoption was sup-posed to remain a secret," she says. "I never did understand why my grandmother told me." She didn't share the information with Erin, however, "because I didn't want [her] to find out we were only half sisters. Somehow I felt she would love me less because of it."

When Heather returned from the visit, she went to see her adop-tive father. "He took me out to breakfast, to reassure me that he still loved me even though I was adopted, and that he was *still* my father. I didn't believe him. He had already lied to me about coming back when I was seven. I loved him with all my heart, but I was angry, hurt and felt I no longer had anything solid under my feet."

Heather is still distant from her adoptive father, although she admits the "best feeling in the world to me would be a great big hug from him, and to *hear* him tell me he loves me." In spite of everything, she adds, "I hold no grudges. Everyone did the best they knew how at the time."

The Birth Parents' Loss

Adoptees aren't the only ones who feel a permanent wound. Their birth parents also suffer, although most suffer quietly. Many in the adoption arena view them as the "invisible members" of the adoption triad. Few hear their views, few look at their feelings and even fewer accept their concerns as genuine.

Thirty-one-year-old "Karen" is just one example. She has a secret tucked away in the recesses of her heart that, she says "will drive me crazy if I I dwell on it." Somewhere out there is an eleven-year-old son she has never met, the product of a rape she would just as soon forget.[6]

Karen was considered to be a very lucky young lady, but when she was twenty, her luck changed. A man she knew as the maintenance man at her apartment complex asked to use the phone. Before he left Karen's apartment, he threatened her life and her roommate's, raped her and left her pregnant.

"I didn't tell anyone," she says, "because I was in shock from the experience. He had already done damage to me, but I didn't want him to hurt my roommate, and I knew that he would. A few months later, I met a man who was kind and gentle, and I thought he was the man I would spend the rest of my life with. We moved in together, and we were very happy."

About four months later Karen learned she was pregnant, but because the couple wanted to get married, they thought everything was fine. Then she had her first prenatal checkup. The doctor said that she was seven months along.

"It didn't make sense to me because I'd had periods every month ... and I wasn't showing until a few weeks before we found out I was pregnant," she says. "When we found out [the truth], my fiancé and I were both devastated. He accused me of being a liar, and I knew it wasn't his baby. He chose to leave me at that time."

Karen went to her family and told them she had been raped and was pregnant with the rapist's child. Fortunately, her family told her that no matter what she decided to do, they would stand by her. She had few options—she couldn't keep a baby conceived during rape, and she was too far along for an abortion—so she decided on adoption. Her mother called the county social services department, and they sent a caseworker to explain the process.

"I was scared to death," she says. "I had all these terrible feelings. Was I doing the right thing? After thinking about it and crying myself to sleep at night, I knew that I was. How could I ever look into the baby's eyes without knowing how it was conceived? It wouldn't be fair. He or she deserved parents who truly loved him or her."

It wasn't as easy as it sounded. Karen had a long, difficult labor that ended in a cesarean section. She remembers looking at her parents' sad faces while she was in labor and feeling helpless.

"I woke up after the delivery, and my dad and brother were standing over me," she says. "Just having people around who loved me helped so much. I had an infection, so I had to stay in the hospital for ten days. I still felt so guilty that I thought [the infection] might somehow be a punishment."

Karen was moved out of the maternity ward and would never have known her baby's sex if the nurses hadn't asked her to sign a consent form for a circumcision. "So I now knew it was a boy," she says, "and that ripped my heart out even more." When she and her fiancé still thought the baby was theirs, they had discussed naming him after Karen's older brother, who was killed in a car wreck four years earlier.

Now Karen struggles to live with the knowledge that "there is an eleven-year-old boy out there somewhere who I hope is happy and healthy." She knows he may try to find her someday, and she is trying to prepare for that day. "If and when that time comes, I have to be strong and remind myself I did the right thing," she says.

JUST WHO ARE BIRTH PARENTS?

"Birth parents," "natural parents," "biological parents," "*real* parents"—just who are these people who give up their children for adoption? Some are women like Karen who had little choice, but almost all feel guilt and grief. And because they signed confidentiality papers at the time of the adoption, many assume they just want to disappear.

That's not necessarily true. Most birth parents can not forget the children they bore as teenagers, and some have banded together to form "search groups" such as Concerned United Birth Parents (CUB), Adoption Triangle Ministry (ATM) and American Adoption Congress (AAC). Too often, they say, birth parents unwillingly signed confidentiality papers when they relinquished their parental rights. Of thousands of CUB birth parents surveyed, only four said they wanted no contact with their relinquished child.[7]

CUB also reports that some birth mothers were bullied into giving up their babies, and Helen remembers being threatened with juvenile hall if she didn't agree to adoption. She wouldn't be cowed, though.

A BIRTH MOTHER WHO SAID "NO"

Helen was sixteen when her son was born. Her father told her she had no choice but adoption, so she went to a maternity home run by Catholic nuns. She remembers feeling guilty for discussing the process with the nuns, and the guilt is still with her today.

Her baby was taken from her at birth and placed in a foster home, but Helen says, "I prayed and prayed. I just couldn't settle with it. I knew in my gut it wasn't right. I cried for six weeks. I kept trying to find a way I could keep him." Finally, she just refused to sign the papers.

"The social worker told me then that nobody could make me sign them. She talked to my dad, and I got my little boy back. When I think of him in that foster home for six weeks it makes me shudder. I still feel so guilty. I wonder what effect that separation had on him." John is thirty-two now and has a child of his own.[8]

Helen's indecisiveness haunted her for thirty-two years. Like Helen, other women believed they would forget their child. It was common for them to be counseled to go on with their lives, "as if giving birth had never happened."

HOW DO YOU FORGET HAVING A CHILD?

"Right!" says Vicki Ransier of Concerned United Birth Parents. "How do you forget something like that? I couldn't do it."

Unwed and sixteen in the 1960s, Ransier was shipped off to a maternity hospital. "I was a 'good girl,' and my parents didn't know what else to do with me," she says. She was a high-school junior dating a football star, and even though her parents pressed for marriage, they said "No."

Ransier and her boyfriend had two "plans" of attack, she said: an abortion clinic in Tijuana, Mexico (abortions were still illegal in the United States), and a maternity home in Ohio. The Mexican abortion ring was broken up just before she got there, which may have been a blessing in disguise. One middle-aged woman, in college in the mid-1960s, remembers driving her best friend from San Francisco to a Tijuana clinic.

"I was only nineteen years old at the time, and I was scared to death," the woman says. "My friend said it would be okay, that she knew another girl who'd gone there. Well, we finally got there, and it was so, so ... sleazy. My friend went in and came out only a short time later. She seemed okay, but shaken, and we started home in my VW. We got only as far as San Diego when she started hemorrhaging all over the car. I took her to the emergency room at the general hospital. I thought she might die.

"Of course, her parents found out then because we had to call for money and for help getting her back home after the bleeding was stopped and an infection was treated. It messed her up for life. She was never able to have children later."[9]

Ransier went to the maternity home in Ohio while her family put on a charade. They told her school, and even her younger brother, that she was ill and had gone to a special climate to recuperate. All alone, with no visitors, Ransier finished her junior year of high school at the Florence Crittenton Maternity Home. There she gave birth to her only son.

"I was real naive and scared, and I had never been away from home," she says. "My boyfriend never told his parents. My parents decided the baby would be adopted. I had no choice, and no counseling. It was a deep, dull secret."[10]

The expectant mothers got no childbirth classes, no preparation for labor, Ransier says. "The girls coming back just said, 'whatever you do, try to relax.' Yeah, right!" She had her son after six and a half hours of hard drug-free labor, then decided as she held him in her arms that she wanted to keep him.

"I spent five days in the hospital taking care of David, and I'm glad I did, but I was used to doing what I was told," she says. "My dad had said I was coming home alone. It was really hard leaving him. The social worker just came in and picked him up and took him off to foster care. I didn't even get to say goodbye."

Ransier went to a foster home after leaving the maternity home, and got periodic reports on her child from her sympathetic foster mother. At five weeks and five days old, she was told, her son was adopted. Like most other birth mothers, however, she simply could not forget her child.

"When he would have been about fifteen, the next-door neighbor kid was about the same age, and I would watch him, thinking about my son," she says. "When you go shopping or drive by schools, you look at the kids, thinking one of them might be [him]."

When he was twenty-five, Ransier's son found her, and they have become fast friends. He found his birth father first, after an extensive search that took several years. "His father almost had a heart attack," she says, "but then he put Mark in touch with me." He shares holidays with Ransier's new family and considers her daughters a new extended family.

Their reunion and her association with other members of Concerned United Birth Parents have helped her come to terms with years of grief, Ransier says. Not all birth parents are that lucky.

MICHELE LAUNDERS

Michele Launders dedicates her book "to Lisa and to birth mothers everywhere." Launders' birth daughter didn't live long enough to be reunited with her. Six-year-old Lisa was killed on November 2, 1987, by Hedda Nussbaum and Joel Steinberg, a couple who had promised to adopt her but never did. She had been illegally adopted by the unmarried couple who were addicted to cocaine and involved in a sadomasochistic relationship. Lisa was starved, battered and sexually abused before her "parents" finally beat her to death.

An estimated four thousand other children died of abuse in America that year, but Lisa Steinberg's death made an imprint on a nation's consciousness. Joyce Johnson covered the Joel Steinberg trial for *Vanity Fair,* and in her book, *What Lisa Knew: The Truths and Lies of the Steinberg Case,* she says of this unfortunate child:

> Lisa was one of those children to whom we assign high value. On the face of it, the middle-aged criminal lawyer and the children's book editor could not have been more appropriate parents. "Why, the Steinbergs are people like us," we said, and we couldn't get over it and get past it. Joel Steinberg and Hedda Nussbaum

showed America and its pregnant teens the meaning
of the word *monster*. When doctors finally disconnected the six-year-old girl from life-support machines,
that monster stepped into our hearts and minds.[11]

Only after Lisa's death did Michele Launders find out who took
her baby home to a life of torture. Until then she thought the child had
been adopted by a wealthy, stable couple. In her book, *I Wish You
Didn't Know My Name: The Story of Michele Launders and Her
Daughter Lisa*, she describes her legacy of remorse:

> You see, I am Lisa's mother. I am the one who brought
> her into the world—and I am the one who inadver-
> tently delivered her into the hands of her abusers. ...
> Lisa's pain is over now. I pray that by writing this book
> I'll find respite from my own.[12]

Only nineteen at the time she signed the relinquishment form for
"Baby Girl Launders," Launders didn't know that Lisa's adoption was never
official. She knew only that she had seen the baby for a few seconds and
then given her to attorney Joel Steinberg. He told her a wealthy Roman
Catholic lawyer and his wife were adopting the child. Launders says she
can't forgive or forget the deception that led to her daughter's death.

After Lisa died, the state of New York passed legislation, known
as the "Lisa Law," that tried to close off the loopholes of private adoption. The law makes it mandatory for prospective parents to start adoption proceedings within ten days of taking a child into their home.
Still, the new law probably wouldn't have thwarted Joel Steinberg,
one family court clerk said. "If you don't bring it to the court's attention that you intend to adopt, there really isn't very much we can do,"
he told Johnson.[13]

Lisa Steinberg, say many present-day teenage mothers, is the reason they would *never* give their child up for adoption. "Look what
happened to her," they say. "It could happen to my child." And birth
mothers who chose adoption worry all the more about the welfare of
the children they relinquished.

Who Is at Risk for Pregnancy?

It is often the young and poor women, those with few alternatives, who suffer the most when faced with an unwanted pregnancy. In the United States, many poor women who are faced with unwanted pregnancies say they feel like "rented wombs" for the more affluent who want their babies. Too often they are right. They take little comfort in the fact that others are profiting from their mistakes, or that they are joined in this tragedy with women in such faraway places as Korea and Romania.

One study has predicted the characteristics of male and female teenagers at risk for single parenthood. The study interviewed people at ages fourteen to twenty-one and found the following patterns:

CHARACTERISTICS OF TEEN PARENTS

- *Criminal records.* About 60 percent of Anglo teenage fathers and half of black and Hispanic teen fathers reported criminal convictions, formal charges not including traffic offenses. Only one-third of nonfathers had brushes with the law.
- *Marijuana use.* Two-thirds of Anglo teen fathers and 57 percent of black and Hispanic fathers used marijuana. Use was 15 points lower for nonfathers.
- *Low income.* Annual family income of teenage fathers' parents was $10,800, compared to $15,600 for nonfathers' parents. A similar pattern emerged for females.
- *Educational problems.* Young women at high risk for pregnancy had disciplinary problems in school, such as cutting class and absenteeism. They also had lower educational aspirations.
- *Depression.* The high-risk girls had instances of depression (20 percent of adolescent girls try to commit suicide).[14]

The latest figures for teenage pregnancy show that more than one million young women between the ages of twelve and nineteen become pregnant each year. Each must decide what is best for them and their children.

One of these young parents is "Joni" of Collingsworth, New Jersey, whose story is recounted in the June 11, 1991, issue of *Women's World* magazine. Joni was fifteen and was impregnated by a rapist. The man jumped out from behind a building one night while she was walking to a friend's house and threw Joni to the ground. She never saw his face.

She felt "sick and dirty," and at first she didn't tell anyone about it. Then she had to face the fact that she was pregnant.[15] "There's no way I'm having this baby!" she screamed at her mother. But an abortion was out of the question for religious reasons.

Joni is also adopted, so to help her decide what to do with her baby, she wrote an open letter to her birth mother. At first she was terrified and repulsed, but now that the baby was kicking and growing, she wrote, "suddenly the baby felt like a part of me. The rape wasn't the baby's fault. I started thinking of her as my little girl." Would she be strong enough to give up her baby?

"Like you, I've tried to imagine an alternative to adoption," Joni wrote. "Maybe Mom could help me raise her; or *I could raise her*. But I always remember I'm just a sophomore in high school. How can I support a child?"[16]

On the other hand, she wrote, how could she give the child up? "I know I'll keep loving her. People might say you can't love someone you never knew—but my baby and I do know each other. She'll always be mine. I know that now."

The Adoption Triad

From one mother's sorrow and pain comes another mother's hope and promise. Like two sides of a coin, their experiences are very opposite—the birth mother and the adoptive mother. Or at least we think they *should* be.

In reality, both have experienced loss—the birth mother has lost her child, the adoptive mother has often lost the possibility of her own natural child, and therefore must turn to someone else to fulfill her dreams.

All members of the adoption triad—birth parents, adoptive parents and their children—must allow the loss to exist so they can understand the past and find comfort in the present. There is no doubt that adoption is necessary, that it was probably necessary for each person in this chapter. Family reunification didn't exist then, and children had physical and emotional needs to be met. In each of these cases, it may not have been the adoption itself which was the true problem, but the mistakes that were unwittingly made in the process, and the consequences of those mistakes. As a nation, we continue to make those mistakes, but it is not a perfect world. We can learn from our mistakes and, as a nation, we must learn.

Conclusions

Just as Russ was adopted thirty-five years ago into a family that was completely different than him, children continue to be placed into families in which it seems clear they will not thrive. They will continue to feel the pain, confusion and hopelessness that Russ feels today.

At first glance, it seems promising that birth mothers are now picking families for their children, and it certainly helps them feel more at ease about their decision to relinquish. Too often, however, they are choosing on the bases of wishes and dreams instead of reality. If this practice is to continue, however, these women must be educated about what makes an adoption successful. The reality is that children do better when matched with parents who are similar in looks, temperament and other genetic variables.

As a society, we have learned from some of our mistakes. We now believe children do better when they know they are adopted, and many open adoptions add to that knowledge by allowing the open exchange of photographs and information as the child grows. All of this will benefit the child and the family. Especially if a child is mismatched, contact with a birth parent can be an enormous benefit and relief.

Birth mothers and fathers who can not forget their absent children are learning that there is hope of reuniting through such organizations as CUB. Many of their children are searching for them, or would like to search if they weren't so afraid. Reuniting can not put back all the years that are gone, but it can be an opening into the future.

Sometimes therapy is an answer for birth parents who can not forget. There may be reasons beyond the adoption that the pain continues. Perhaps the parent has issues about her own childhood that, once exposed and examined, would free her from the past.

All members of the adoption triad would do well to remember what CBS News correspondent (and adopted child) Faith Daniels told the Congressional Coalition on Adoption several years ago. "Adoption is not a detriment," she said. "Being an orphan is!"[17]

Adoption should not be a detriment, and in many cases it is not. But we must understand the reasons that adoptions are successful and make the changes which are necessary so that we do not have to face adopted children in the future who tell us, "I just couldn't be who they wanted me to be."

---

[1] "Russ," personal interview, Los Angeles, California, 1989.

[2] "Richard," personal interview, California, 1989.

[3] Walter Conley, personal interview, Denver, Colorado, April 1991.

[4] Joan Keres, personal interview, Denver, Colorado, April 1992.

[5] Heather McKelvey, personal interview, San Francisco, California, July 1992.

[6] "Karen,"personal interview, Denver, Colorado, 1990.

[7] E. Lynn Giddens, *Faces of Adoption,* 1984, p. 44.

[8] Helen, personal interview, April 1991.

[9] Anonymous, personal interview, April 17, 1991.

[10] Vicki Ransier, personal interview, Wheat Ridge, Colorado, January 1991.

[11] Joyce Johnson, *What Lisa Knew: The Truths and Lies of the Steinberg Case* (New York: Putnam, 1990): p. 39.

[12] Michele Launders and Penina Spiegel, *I Wish You Didn't Know My Name: The Story of Michele Launders and Her Daughter Lisa,* Batfilm Productions, Warner Books, 1990.

[13] Johnson, *What Lisa Knew,* p. 48.

[14] The *Ms.* Foundation for Women, August 1991.

[15] "There's No Way I'm Having This Baby!" *Women's World* (June 11, 1991).

[16] Ibid., p. 17.

[17] Eileen Putman, Associated Press, April 26, 1987.

CONCLUSIONS

CHAPTER TWELVE

CLOSING THOUGHTS

> *Every beetle is like a*
> *Gazelle in the eyes of its mother.*
> Moorish Proverb

It is time in America to face the truth about our child welfare system or suffer the consequences. The truth: It is a system that is grossly inadequate for the job that it has been assigned to do. The consequences: Hundreds of thousands of children spend their lives in limbo.

Solutions are another thing altogether, and not nearly as simple to define. Some require only small changes in the system—revised requirements for adoptive parents, national systems to keep adoption statistics, etc. Others call for a major overhaul. Dixie van de Flier Davis, director of the Rocky Mountain Adoption Exchange, would like to see at least as much money spent on adoption and family preservation as we spend on foster care. While she's at it, she would like to see the foster care budget *redirected* into the adoption system.

"The resources and the money are there in the foster care system," she says. "We need to shift that money to a place where it makes sense, where it will foster permanency in these children's lives."[1]

Her proposal is based on the assumption that the many severely scarred children waiting for homes can, with careful assessment, treatment and care, fit into a loving family. When that's possible, they deserve the chance to succeed. But this approach requires that potential adoptive parents be reeducated about the kinds of children who are available to them, what to expect from these children and how they can deal with it. That involves more preadoption training than is presently available.

As Susan Cox, Director of Development at Holt International Children's Services in Eugene, Oregon, so aptly puts it, "Those of us who advocate for all waiting children need to remind those who might forget that the purpose of adoption is to find families for children, not children for families."

Adoptive parents aren't the only ones who need reeducation. Adoption agencies also need new information about who qualifies as "proper" parents. Artificial roadblocks such as marital status, age and ability to pay fees have stalled numerous parents who were eager to adopt.

"Why have charges to adopt?" asks Davis. "If we are truly looking out for the children's interests, and we are asking families to take them into their lives, children who are going to need extensive psychological treatment ... why should we also ask them to pay for it?"[2]

Some progress has been made. In 1986, the U.S. Congress approved the National Adoption Information Clearinghouse as part of the Department of Health and Human Services. Its purpose was to make it easier to match waiting adoptive parents and waiting children, but already it is behind schedule. The legislation mandated that the national reporting system be up and running by October, 1991, and more than two years later it was still on the drawing board.

We urge them to follow through, not just so that children can be matched with parents but also because such record keeping will provide statistical information about disruption rates. Researchers can then comb the data for clues about why some adoptions work and others don't. They may also be able to make a case for the kind of postadoption support that boosts success rates.

For whether we like it or not, adoption is a profound experience that proves unsettling for every member of the triad—the birth parents who have lost a child, the child who has lost his genetic family and the adoptive parents who have lost the "fantasy child" they might have conceived themselves.[3]

Throughout *Adoption Crisis*, the reader has found stories of adoptive parents who have had the courage to speak candidly; some of them have had years of frustration and others have been rewarded for their efforts with children who finally found their way home. Without the courage of these parents, there would be no story to tell.

The reader has also found compelling evidence that genetics and temperament play an enormous role in the success of an adoption. It seems appropriate to repeat that thought here.

Scientists are taking a harder look at the influence genetics have on a child's temperament. As we have discussed, personality disorders, alcoholism and mental illnesses such as manic depression and schizophrenia have been demonstrated to run in families. New evidence suggests that these traits are passed on through chromosomes.

We don't know just how many personality features are passed down through genetics, nor do we know whether it is the predisposition for mental illness that is passed on or simply personality traits that develop into illness in the right kind of environment. We do not really know if these are "fragile genetics" or sound genetics that erode due to environmental problems.

Evidence is building that genetics are predominant. In fact, results of a study released in April, 1993, show that a person's vulnerability to stress may be inherited. A study of more than eight thousand twins who served in the military in the Vietnam War era showed that some had an inherited vulnerability to post-traumatic stress disorder.[4]

Others studies, including a landmark study of twins reared apart done by the University of Michigan, indicate that 70 percent of our intelligence is inherited, making it far more influential than the contributions of schools and family environment. Authors of that study note, "Nothing in the study tells us that intervention is not a possibility, but we have to pay attention to the unique talents of each child." For the researchers, the study settled "the IQ issue for most people."[5]

Because science has established once and for all that temperament plays a major role in who we will be as adults, we believe that it is only when parents are successfully matched with their adoptive children that the strength of "nurture" can complement what "nature" has already provided. Adoptive parents must insist that this temperament testing be done, and agencies must do what is necessary to prevent mismatches.

Anytime a child is placed in foster care, the same matching issues need to be considered. Even though the placement is intended to be short term, weeks have a way of turning into years, and children may end up spending their entire childhoods with foster parents who have no real understanding of who they are.

In this interest, we have developed the Stevens Adopt-Match Evaluator (SAME), an instrument now being tested by agencies involved with adoption and challenged children. The SAME should provide the type of information needed to make certain that adoptive families are compatible. Although no one can guarantee success with an adoption, it is certainly prudent to use all the tools available before taking this plunge.

Such information is doubly important for the growing group of children with special needs—those who are older, members of a sibling group or minority group and those with special physical, educational and emotional challenges. Some of these children are shuffled from one foster home to another, or from one disrupted adoption to another, partly because their families are unaware of the extent of the children's problems and are not taught how to deal with them. When children have had three disruptions, their chances for successful adoption are usually over. They are considered unadoptable, unable to form a bond with parents, and they are transferred to residential treatment facilities at enormous financial and emotional cost to the nation.

Adoptions are failing in record numbers, with some estimating that up to 75 percent of all special-needs adoptions fail.[6] Experts agree this doesn't have to happen. If these youngsters are identified early, given proper treatment and quickly matched with appropriate parents, their chances of success are greatly enhanced. When the American child welfare system is capable of doing *that,* it will indeed be a great day.

■   ■   ■

As a society, we must come to our senses and redesign a system that will work toward providing loving, secure homes for every child. Their lives should be filled with wonder, not overcome by wondering what will become of them.

It will be less expensive in the long run to provide their families with services that "strengthen and support" them before they split apart. Rather than charging crack-addicted mothers with child abuse, for example, we could start by trying to teach them how to defeat their addictions and hold their families together. The Homebuilders program has shown that some can succeed with intensive intervention and support services.

When that doesn't work, we can respond by giving their children the best substitute families we can find. Adoptive parents and case-workers must take up the gauntlet in this battle and be on the front lines to unite and educate the public, but the efforts of all segments of society are required if there is to be meaningful change. There are many solutions to the problems of our unwanted children, but they will take a ground swell of grass-roots support to accomplish.

It is with knowledge and conviction that adoptive relationships can grow and mature. It is also important to remember the old adage:

To change the world, start by changing just one child.

---

[1] Dixie van de Flier Davis, personal interview, Denver, Colorado, 1991.
[2] Ibid.
[3] The North American Council on Adoptable Children, *Adoptalk* (Summer 1991): p. 1.
[4] William True, *Archives of General Psychiatry* (April 1993).
[5] Gina Kolata, quoting Dr. Thomas Bouchard, *New York Times/Denver Post,* October 12, 1990, p. 8.
[6] "Child Protection Report," 1984.

APPENDICES

STRATEGIES FOR ADOPTIVE PARENTS

Just what process must an adoptive parent go through to find a child he can live with? According to the Child Welfare League of America, it is the "primary purpose of an adoption service ... to help children who would not otherwise have a home of their own, and who can benefit from family life, to become members of a family that can give them the love, care, protection and opportunities essential for their healthy personal growth and development."[1] For various reasons outlined in this book, this hasn't been the case.

We offer these cautions and guidelines for those seeking a child:

Adoptive parents must be cautious when pursuing adoption, whether through a state agency, private agency or a private adoption. Know the costs up front and the criteria you must meet.

Have realistic expectations and realize that as adopting parents, you may not get your "fantasy child." See how realistic it is for you to stretch your expectations.

Generally, you can adopt through both public and private agencies. In some states, however, only private agencies handle children who are free for adoption. For more information, check with the state agencies in your location.

Private agencies generally are more expensive, but their criteria may not be as difficult to meet. If you have questions about agencies and their practices, check with the National Committee for Adoption, 2025 M St. NW, Washington, DC 20036; (202) 463-7559.

Agency Adoption

Given the system under which adoptions and foster care operate in this country, an agency adoption is often the only way a family can get a child. Public agencies handle both healthy infants and children with special needs.

Most agencies have very long waiting lists for healthy infants, so families also are often told to wait before applying and beginning a home study. Don't be put off by perfunctory first answers. Should you be interested in only a healthy infant, continue to ask questions, even if the agency says they have a long waiting list or aren't taking applications. Don't be frightened away. Ask when the list will be opened and when you can fill out an application. If not now, when?

Some agencies also have what is called a "modified designated adoption program," in which birth parents can choose adoptive parents from a pool of couples who have completed their home studies. If the birth parents feel a family is right for their child, the wait can be shortened. One drawback is that many birth parents are uninformed about making such choices and may not do well for their children. A better system uses matching tests to determine which prospective family is best suited to each child.

Children who are older, of color, part of a sibling group or who have physical, mental or emotional challenges fall into the "special-needs" category. Parents interested in adopting them can apply for an immediate home study to approve the family for adoption. After the study is complete, the family can begin pressing the agency for a child who will be a good match for the family.

Many counties also hold "adoption fairs" where most agencies—public and private—are represented to attract potential adoptive parents and answer questions. Many agencies also provide a book of "waiting children" that can be viewed by prospective parents. Expect to look at pictures and brief information on about thirty children. Ask yourself how far you can "stretch" to provide a safe environment for one of these needy children. Be honest with yourself about your abilities and expectations.

Most agencies hold orientation meetings to go over information about policies and requirements. This gives potential adoptive parents the information they need to determine if they really want to adopt. The agency will most likely require information about:

- *Other children in the home.* Most agencies prefer to serve those with infertility problems, but agencies may encourage families to adopt a second child so children will have siblings.
- *Age.* Agencies generally look for parents who are no more than forty years older than the child being adopted. This rule is ostensibly to ensure a long and happy relationship.
- *Marital status.* Most agencies place babies only with married couples. Since there are so many qualified infertile couples seeking to adopt (about fifty to one hundred per each available healthy baby), agencies prefer two-parent families. Most birth mothers also express a desire that their babies be adopted by married couples.
- *Health.* Medical reports are usually requested. Agencies seek healthy, though not perfect, adoptive parents.
- *An acceptable house.* Agencies do not require parents to own a home, only that they be capable of providing a good environment for the child.
- *Religion.* Adoption agencies affiliated with sectarian organizations, such as Baptist, Catholic, Jewish or Mormon, frequently serve members of their own faith on a priority basis.
- *Employment.* Some agencies prefer that one parent stay at home with the newly adopted child for at least several months. (Since the Family Leave Act passed in 1993, some new parents are eligible for maternity-leave benefits.) Other agencies will consider two-career families if they have an appropriate day-care plan.
- *Income.* Agencies will often look at recent tax returns or other financial information to make sure parents are in a position to adequately provide for the child. They are more interested in how the income is managed than how much income is earned.[2]

If the experience with an agency is discouraging, don't stop there. Contact the state or regional Adoption Exchange Service (see the listing in Appendix III) and explore the option of being listed there as an available family.

Private Adoption

After trying the agency route for awhile, some adoptive couples come to the conclusion that they will have to find a child privately. Most states allow such adoptions through a qualified attorney, but be careful. There are pitfalls, and this route can be emotionally and financially draining.

Usually the birth parent is responsible for selecting a specific family, often "introduced" to them by an intermediary, such as a lawyer, minister, doctor or friend, who brings the parties together. Private agencies counsel the parties involved, and adoptive parents are studied and approved or rejected. (For the best chances of a successful private adoption, please refer to the information on "mediated adoption" in Appendix III.)

It is possible to do a private adoption without an agency, but the law requires a home study to be done and legal proceedings completed before the adoption can be finalized. That process involves:

1. Placement.
2. Postplacement—in most states this means caseworkers must submit periodic reports to the court on the progress of the child within the new family. This is the "honeymoon" period in which the child and family adjust to each other, usually lasting six months to one year. It can be one of the most difficult periods, and it is usually advisable that an agency, caseworker, parent group and/or professional counselor assist the family during this time.
3. Finalization—the agency or an attorney of the family's choice will accompany the parents to court for the legal actions.
4. Postfinalization—during this time it is important to have a counselor working with the family to help with the adjustment. When the adoptee is a special-needs child, professional counseling is especially important.

Some private agencies clearly promote "open adoption," a fairly new process that allows interaction among birth parents, adoptive parents and the child. Open adoption flies in the face of old adoption policies that urged birth parents to pretend their children never existed and told adoptive parents to treat the children as if they were born to them. Those methods proved to be harmful, and now the vast majority of all adoptive parents tell their children that they are adopted, more than half doing so before the children turn three.

These disclosures have led most adoption professionals today to agree that adoptees need to know basic facts about their birth parents, and it is in this atmosphere that open adoption has evolved. Some agencies allow birth mothers to handpick their children's adoptive parents. The most common process involves compiling a booklet with photographs and descriptions of couples interested in adopting, and allowing birth mothers to choose one couple from the book to interview.

It is too early to determine whether children involved in open adoption are healthier or happier because of it. Experts assume success depends on how the open adoption was handled. Birth mothers suffer if they discover they have been manipulated and promised things that don't materialize, and their children also feel the strain of that deception.

International Adoption

A wider range of children may be available in foreign countries than in the United States. An international agency usually acts as the go-between and arranges for the home study and adoption approval. (See Appendix III for a list of international agencies.)

Adopting Children

We turned to the experts for step-by-step information about how to adopt.

ADOPTION OF AN INFANT

It would be wise to follow the same steps for any child under two years old if the birth parents are available.

Initial contact
Home study
Preadoption counseling
Matching personalities and temperaments of two parent groups (prior to birth if possible)
Assess child's freedom for adoption (have consent forms signed by both birth parents)
Check on prenatal screening and counseling of the birth mother
Genetic counseling (for inherited medical disorders, abnormalities or drug/alcohol use during pregnancy)
Newborn screening and diagnosis (Apgar test and Brazelton Neonatal)
Birth and congenital history
Plan for follow-up
Postadoption counseling

ADOPTION OF A CHILD OVER AGE TWO

These steps are advisable when adopting any child over two years old.

Initial contact
Home study
Preadoption counseling
Matching with child (and parents if available) before any meeting with the child
If child is free, have consent forms signed by both parents
Receive Life Book of early care
Full disclosure of congenital information, abuse or neglect
History of placements and reasons for changes
Medical history
Psychological history
Careful assessment of special needs
Any training to manage special needs
Plan for follow-up and postadoption counseling

HIV-POSITIVE, AIDS OR DRUG-EXPOSED BABIES

Check all items regarding adoption of an infant and/or child over two. Also, determine what possible financial help might be available. In addition to the above, follow these guidelines:

Special screening and diagnosis
Training in medical care
Training in psychological care
Family therapy around the issues of adopting such a child, which should
  be resolved and worked out

Regardless of which process is chosen, every adoptive child comes with a history, and many can come with challenges. In the past, adoption agencies have been reluctant to disclose them for fear of "self-fulfilling prophesies." They worry that adoptive parents will label their children if they have all the facts. This can happen, but the consequences of not knowing a child's history can be just as bad or worse.

The lucky few who can adopt an infant must spend the first year working on the bonding process. Infants bond more easily than older children, but they still experience problems. For more information on how to bond and attach to a child, please see the resource section in Appendix III.

There are some things adoptive families *have to know* if they are to cope with crises as they arise, including:

- The truth about the child, no matter how awful.
- What this truth means for the child's future. Will she have an attachment disorder or emotional problems? If so, how will these affect her life and the family's?
- The kinds of problems the adoption will entail.
- What kind of therapy the child will need and how much it is expected to cost.

The agency *should* provide:

- Comprehensive assessment work, including gathering genetic and congenital information for every child entering the system. This will be particularly hard to obtain for children who have been abused, neglected or abandoned prior to adoption.
- Full disclosure of their findings to prospective families. Drug use during pregnancy is especially difficult to document, and prospective parents need to know that.

Social workers under staggering caseloads can enlist the help of the parents in tracking down the child's history. When the prospective family gets involved with researching records and talking to a geneticist about the implications of the child's history, it is possible to forge a partnership with the agency. It is also likely to draw them closer to the potential adopted child and her problems.

A child's records can make all the difference in a successful adoption. Some examples:

- A birth mother can write a letter describing the cute, endearing things the child did as a baby and the reasons why she could no longer care for him. This can help the child understand the birth mother's situation and realize that he did not cause the separation.
- The orphanage director or foster families can keep histories with pictures and records of the child's feelings while in their care. This is called a Life Book.
- Adoptive parents can use these records to help the child understand the placements and deal with hurt feelings acquired along the way. It will help the parent and child work through the grieving process.

---

[1] Child Welfare League of America, *The Standards for Adoption Service*, New York.
[2] National Committee for Adoption, *Adoption Factbook*, 1989, pp. 161–62.

THE STEVENS ADOPT-MATCH EVALUATOR (SAME)

This test instrument is the first of its kind to actually measure the compatibility of an adoptive child with his potential parents. It has been developed as part of a screening battery for adoption workers and psychologists to use in forging a compatible "family fit." Of course, no simple solutions exist which can guarantee such a fit, but with diligent homework and the use of such instruments, adoption workers can satisfy themselves and their clients that they have done everything possible to assure a successful adoption.

This test instrument has also been found useful in the evaluation of "family fit" problems after adoption. It can help identify the sources of problems between the adoptive child and his parents. Once these problems are identified, work can be done to improve the situation. The SAME, used in conjunction with pre- and postadoption services and follow-up, should give each family the knowledge it needs to succeed.

TEST SAMPLE: (ADULT EVALUATOR)

1. My tendency is to
   a. plan things ahead of time
   b. do things spontaneously

2. I have a hard time
   a. doing something I don't want to do
   b. admitting my faults

3. It is better to
   a. have the right answers
   b. be able to imagine

4. I find it easier to understand
   a. things I know inside me
   b. things I can see around me

5. I am usually
   a. sociable
   b. private

TEST SAMPLE: (CHILD EVALUATOR)

1. I love to
   a. dream and pretend
   b. play

2. Walking up and talking to people I don't know is
   a. hard
   b. easy

3. I don't like
   a. my friends playing with anyone but me
   b. not knowing what is going to happen next

4. Sometimes I
   a. feel silly
   b. feel scared

5. I like to have
   a. lots of friends
   b. one best friend

The complete Stevens Adopt-Match Evaluator is available to qualified administrators by writing Dr. Howard Stevens and Dr. JoEllen Stevens, P.O. Box 1133, Oakview, CA 93022. Administration and evaluation services are also available.

The authors recommend that the SAME be used in conjunction with a complete battery of tests, outlined in the following pages, for a comprehensive evaluation.

BATTERY FOR ADOPTION PROFILE

I. For Infants.

If birth parents (A and B)* and adopting parents (C and D)* are available, evaluate all four with:

1. WAIS-R/WISC-R (Wechsler Adult Intelligence Scale-Revised/ Wechsler Intelligence Scale for Children-Revised)
2. Stevens Adopt-Match Evaluator (SAME) for adults
3. Physical/cultural characteristics checklist (race, ethnic background, family physical characteristics)
4. Clinical interview

II. For Children over One and One Half Years of Age.

If birth parents (A and B) and adopting parents (C and D) are available, evaluate all four plus the child.

Evaluate parents with:

1. WAIS-R/WISC-R
2. Stevens Adopt-Match Evaluator for adults
3. Physical/cultural characteristics checklist
4. Clinical interview

Evaluate child with:

1. WIPPSI or WISC-R (if age is appropriate)
2. Physical/cultural characteristics checklist
3. Clinical observation

III. For Children Five Years of Age and Older.**

If birth parents (A and B) and adopting parents (C and D) are available, evaluate all four plus the child.

Evaluate parents with:

1. WAIS-R/WISC-R
2. Stevens Adopt-Match Evaluator for adults
3. Physical/cultural characteristics checklist
4. Clinical interview

Evaluate child with:

1. WIPPSI (Wechsler Preschool and Primary Scale of Intelligence) or WISC-R (if age is appropriate)
2. Stevens Adopt-Match Evaluator for children
3 Physical/cultural characteristics checklist
4. Clinical observation and/or interview

    * A - birth mother   * C - adoptive mother
    * B - birth father   * D - adoptive father

** Children age four may be evaluated with this method if it is deemed appropriate.

APPENDIX III

RESOURCES

Other Sources of Information

Attachment Disorders and Therapy

ATTACh Network, c/o Barbara Rila, 2775 Villa Creek, Suite 240, Dallas, TX 75234.

Attachment Center at Evergreen, P.O. Box 2764, Evergreen, CO 80439.

Attachment Disorders Parents Network, Gail Trenberth, P.O. Box 18475, Boulder, CO 80308.

Dr. Foster Cline, Evergreen Consultants in Human Behavior, Evergreen, CO 80439.

Connell Watkins and Associates, Evergreen, CO; (303) 674-6860.

Foreign Adoption

International Concerns Committee for Children, 911 Cypress Dr., Boulder, CO 80303; (303) 494-8333. "Report on Foreign Adoption, 1993," $20.

Genetic Services

Adoption Worker's Guide to Genetic Services, Rauch & Rike, University of Maryland, School of Social Work and Community Planning, Baltimore.

Legislation Regarding Women's and Children's Issues

Rep. Patricia Schroeder, United States Congress, House of Representatives, Washington, DC 10515.

Mediated Open Adoption

Jeanne Etter, Adoption Mediation Seminars, 85444 Teague Loop, Eugene, OR 97405.

Parenting Drug Babies

Debbe Magnusen at the Cuddle Project, Inc., for information about the Cuddle-Wrap swaddling device for drug-addicted or premature infants, 209 Technology Dr., Suite 200, Irvine, CA 92718. Magnusen's book, *It's Never Dull*, is also available.

Intricate Love: A First-Year Guide to Parenting Infants Affected by Substance Abuse, Kimm E. Bolding, Pikes Peak Foster Adopt Resources, Inc., P.O. Box 359, Colorado Springs, CO 80901.

Postadoption Services

North American Council on Adoptable Children (NACAC), eight-week curriculum "Family Preservation: The Second Time Around," 1821 University Ave., Suite N-498, St. Paul, MN 55104.

RESOURCES FOR FINDING BIRTH PARENTS AND CHILDREN

There are numerous resources available for those who are searching for their heritage. The most prominent are ALMA (Adoptees' Liberty Movement Association), Adoptees in Search and CUB (Concerned United Birth Parents), founded by birth parents. Chapters of these organizations exist in most states to help adoptive children and biological parents locate each other. Their headquarters and other search groups follow:

- ALMA. Adoptees' Liberty Movement Association, P.O. Box 154, Washington Bridge Station, New York, NY 10033; (212) 581-1568.
- CUB. Concerned United Birth Parents, 2000 Walker St., Des Moines, IA 50317.

- International Soundex Reunion Registry, P.O. Box 2312, Carson City, NV 89702-2312.
- Triadoption Library, Inc., c/o Mary Jo Rillera, P.O. Box 638, Westminster, CA 92684.

Information on searching for and opening of adoption records can be obtained from the following publication:

- Adoption Registry Packet, National Committee for Adoption (NCFA), 1930 Seventeenth St. NW, Washington, DC 20009. Includes a copy of NCFA's "Model Act on Mutual Consent Registries" and a list of state laws.

Agencies Helping Adopting Parents

Most of this listing comes from the National Committee for Adoption in Washington, D.C. The authors gratefully acknowledge the agency's contribution. NCFA members represent more than one hundred adoption or maternity service agencies throughout the United States. Most of them are nonprofit, volunteer organizations. The authors have added some resource agencies and groups they encountered while writing *Adoption Crisis.*

UNITED STATES

Alabama

State Agency: Alabama State Department of Human Resources, 64 N. Union St., Montgomery, AL 36130; (205) 261-3409.
Lifeline Children's Services, 2908 Pump House Rd., Birmingham, AL 35243; (205) 967-0811.

Alaska

State Agency: Alaska Department of Health and Social Services, Division of Family and Youth Services, Pouch H-05, Juneau, AK 99811; (907) 465-3631.
State Exchange: same as above.

Latter-Day Saints (LDS) Social Services Alaska Office, Alaska Mutual
   Bank Building, 4020 De Barr St., #225A, Anchorage, AK 99508;
   (907) 337-6696.

Arizona

State Agency: Arizona Department of Economic Security, State Adop-
   tion Registry, 1400 W. Washington, Phoenix, AZ 85009; (602)
   255-3981.
State Exchange: P.O. Box 17951, Tucson, AZ 85731; (602) 327-3324.
Aid for Adoption of Special Kids, 1611 E. Camelback, Suite 8, Phoe-
   nix, AZ 85016; (602) 262-2863.
LDS Social Services Mesa Office, 235 S. El Dorado, Mesa, AZ 85202;
   (602) 968-2995.
LDS Social Services Page Office, P.O. Box 3544, Page, AZ 86040; (602)
   645-2489.
LDS Social Services Snowflake Office, P.O. Box 856, 601 South Main
   St., Snowflake, AZ 85937; (602) 536-4117.
LDS Social Services Tucson Office, 3535 S. Richey, Tucson, AZ 85713;
   (602) 745-6459.

Arkansas

State Agency: Arkansas Department of Human Services, Division of
   Children and Family Services, P.O. Box 1437, Little Rock, AR
   72207; (501) 371-2207.
State Exchange: same as above.
Adoption Services, Inc., 2415 N. Tyler, Little Rock, AR 72207; (501)
   664-0340.
Catholic Social Services, 2415 N. Tyler, Little Rock, AR 72207; (501)
   664-0340.
For the Love of Children, 217 W. Second St., Little Rock, AR 72201;
   (501) 378-0225.

California

State Agency: Adoptions Branch, California Department of Social Services, 744 P St., Sacramento, CA 95814; (916) 322-5973.

No State Exchange.

Aid for Adoption of Special Kids, 2081 Business Center Dr., #188, Irvine, CA 92715; (714) 752-8305.

Bethany Christian Services, Unit #1, 9556 Flower, Bellflower, CA 90706; (213) 804-3448.

Bethany Christian Services, 2937 Veneman, Suite 265C, Modesto, CA 95356; (209) 522-5121.

LDS Social Services Anaheim Office, 501 N. Brookhurst, #300, Anaheim, CA 92801; (714) 824-8480.

LDS Social Services Colton Office, 791 N. Pepper Ave., Colton, CA 92324; (714) 824-0480.

LDS Social Services Fremont Office, 37541 Blacow Rd., Fremont, CA 94536; (415) 790-1800.

LDS Social Services Fresno Office, 2686 S. Maple, Fresno, CA 93725; (209) 441-8022.

LDS Social Services Sacramento Office, 3000 Auburn Blvd., Suite 1, Sacramento, CA 95821; (916) 971-3555.

LDS Social Services San Diego Office, 5464 Grossmont Center Dr., Suite #330, La Mesa, CA 92042; (619) 466-5558.

LDS Social Services Van Nuys Office, 7100 Hayvenhurst Ave., #102, Van Nuys, CA 91406; (818) 781-5511.

LDS Social Services Ventura Office, 3585 Maple St., Suite 256, Ventura, CA 93004; (805) 642-0338.

Colorado

State Agency: Colorado Department of Social Services, 717 17th St., P.O. Box 18100, Denver, CO 80218-0899; (303) 294-5962 or 2859.

Bethany Christian Services, 2140 S. Ivanhoe, Suite 106, Denver, CO 80222; (303) 758-4484.

Hand-in-Hand International Adoptions, 1617 W. Colorado Ave., Colorado Springs, CO 80904; (719) 473-8844.

LDS Social Services, 3263 Fraser St., Suite 3, Aurora, CO 80011; (303) 371-1000.

Rocky Mountain Adoption Exchange, 925 S. Niagara, Suite 100, Denver CO 80224; (303) 321-9747.

Connecticut

State Agency: Department of Children and Youth Services, Connecticut Adoption Resource Exchange, 170 Sigourney St., Hartford, CT 06105; (203) 566-8742.

State Exchange: same as above.

Delaware

State Agency: Adoption Services Coordinator, Delaware Division of Child Protective Services, 330 E. 30th St., Wilmington, DE 19802; (302) 571-6419.

District of Columbia

Public Agency: Adoption and Placement Resources Branch, District of Columbia Department of Human Services, 500 1st St. NW, Washington, DC 20001; (202) 727-3161.

No State Exchange.

Adoption Services Information Agency (ASIA), 7720 Alaska Ave. NW, Washington, DC 20012; (202) 726-7193.

The Barker Foundation, 4114 River Rd. NW, Washington, DC 20016; (202) 363-7751.

Florida

State Agency: Florida Department of Health and Rehabilitation Services, Children, Youth and Families, 1317 Winewood Blvd., Tallahassee, FL 32301; (904) 488-8000.

State Exchange: same as above.

Florida Baptist Children's Home, P.O. Box 8190, Lakeland, FL 33802; (813) 687-8811.

LDS Social Services, 1020 N. Orlando Ave., Suite F, Winter Park, FL 32789; (407) 628-8899.

Shepard Care Ministries, Inc., 5935 Taft St., Suite B, Hollywood, FL 33021; (305) 981-2060.

Georgia

State Agency: Adoption Unit, Georgia Department of Human Resources, 878 Peachtree St. NE, Atlanta, GA 30309; (404) 894-4456.

State Exchange: same as above.

Bethany Christian Services, 682 Mulberry, Macon, GA 31201; (912) 742-6964.

LDS Social Services, 4823 N. Royal Atlanta Dr., Tucker, GA 30084; (404) 939-2121.

Open Door Adoption Agency, P.O. Box 4, Thomasville, GA 31799; (912) 228-6339.

Hawaii

State Agency: Hawaii Department of Social Services and Housing, Family and Children's Services, 1149 Bethel St., Honolulu, HI 96813; (808) 548-6739.

No State Exchange.

LDS Social Services, 1500 S. Beretania St., #403, Honolulu, HI 96826; (808) 945-3690.

Idaho

State Agency: Idaho Department of Health and Welfare, 450 N. State, Boise, ID 83720; (208) 334-3546.

State Exchange: same as above.

America's Children, P.O. Box 1000, Boise, ID 83701; (208) 773-0526.

Catholic Counseling Services, 545 Shoup Ave., Idaho Falls, ID 83402; (208) 529-4673.

LDS Social Services, 10740 Fairview, Boise, ID 83704; (208) 376-0191.

Illinois

State Agency: Illinois Department of Children and Family Services, Office of Adoptions, 100 W. Randolph, Chicago, IL 60601.

State Exchange: (for adoption information), Adoption Information Center of Illinois, 201 N. Wells St., Suite 1342, Chicago, IL 60606; (312) 346-1516.

Catholic Charities of Chicago, 126 N. Des Plaines, Chicago, IL 60606; (312) 236-5172.

LDS Social Services, 1813 N. Mill St., Naperville, IL 60540; (312) 369-0486.

Indiana

State Agency: Indiana Department of Public Welfare, Child Welfare–Social Services Division, 141 S. Meridian St., Indianapolis, IN 46225; (317) 232-4434.

State Exchange: Indiana Adoption Resource Exchange, same as above.

Adoptions Resource Services, 810 W. Bristol, Elkhart, IN 46514; (219) 626-2497.

Bethany Christian Services, 9595 Whitley Dr., Indianapolis, IN 46240; (317) 848-9518.

Catholic Family Services, 524 Franklin Square, Michigan City, IN 46360; (219) 879-9312.

Iowa

State Agency: Iowa Department of Human Services, Hoover State Office Building, Des Moines, IA 50319; (515) 281-5358.

Kansas

State Agency: Youth Services, Kansas State Department of Social and Rehabilitation Services, 2700 W. 6th St., Topeka, KS 66606; (913) 296-4661.

State Exchange: same as above.

Kentucky

State Agency: Cabinet for Human Resources, Kentucky Department for Social Services, 275 E. Main St., Frankfort, KY 40601; (502) 564-2136.

State Exchange: Kentucky Adoption Resource Exchange, same as above.
SNAP (Special Needs Adoption Project), 710 W. High St., Lexington, KY 40508; (606) 252-1728.

Louisiana

State Agency: Louisiana Department of Health and Human Resources, Office of Human Development, Division of Children, Youth and Family Services, P.O. Box 3318, Baton Rouge, LA 70821; (504) 342-4040.
State Exchange: Louisiana Adoption Resource Exchange, address same as above; (504) 342-4041.

Maine

State Agency: Maine Department of Human Services, Bureau of Social Services, 221 State St., Augusta, ME 04333; (207) 289-2971.

Maryland

State Agency: Maryland Adoption Resource Exchange, Social Services Administration, 300 W. Preston St., Baltimore, MD 21201; (301) 576-5313.
State Exchange: same as above.

Massachusetts

State Agency: Massachusetts Department of Social Services, 150 Causeway St., Boston, MA 02114; (617) 727-0900.
State Exchange: Massachusetts Adoption Resource Exchange, 867 Boylston St., Boston, MA 02116; (617) 536-0362.

Michigan

State Agency: Michigan Department of Social Services, Office of Children and Youth Services, 300 S. Capitol Ave., P.O. Box 30037, Lansing, MI 48909; (517) 373-3513.

State Exchange: Michigan Adoption Resource Exchange, same as above.

Minnesota

State Agency: Adoption Unit, Minnesota Department of Human Services, Centennial Building, St. Paul, MN 55155; (612) 296-3740.
State Exchange: Minnesota State Adoption Exchange, same as above.

Mississippi

State Agency: Mississippi State Department of Public Welfare. P.O. Box 352, Jackson, MS 39205; (601) 354-0341.
State Exchange: Mississippi Adoption Resource Exchange, same as above.

Missouri

State Agency: Missouri Department of Social Services, Division of Family Services, P.O. Box 88, Jefferson City, MO 65103; (314) 751-2981.
No State Exchange.

Montana

State Agency: Montana State Community Services, Box 4210, Helena, MT 59604; (406) 444-3865.
Rocky Mountain Adoption Exchange, see Colorado.

Nebraska

State Agency: Nebraska Department of Social Services, P.O. Box 95026, Lincoln, NB 68509; (402) 471-3121.
State Exchange: Adoption Exchange Service of Nebraska, same as above.

Nevada

State Agency: Nevada State Welfare Division, Department of Human Resources, 2527 N. Carson St., Carson City, NV 89710; (702) 885-3023.

State Exchange: same as above.

New Hampshire

State Agency: New Hampshire Division for Children and Youth Services, Hazen Dr., Concord, NH 03301; (603) 271-3602.

New Jersey

State Agency: New Jersey Division of Youth and Family Services, Adoption Unit, CN 717, 1 S. Montgomery St., Trenton, NJ 08625; (609) 633-6991.

New Mexico

State Agency: New Mexico Department of Human Services, P.O. Box 2348, Santa Fe, NM 87503-2348; (505) 827-4109.

New York

State Agency: New York State Department of Social Services, Adoption Services, 40 N. Pearl St., Albany, NY 12243; (518) 474-2868.

No State Exchange.

Adoption and Counseling Service, Inc., One Fayette Park, Syracuse, NY 13202; (315) 471-0109.

Catholic Charities of Buffalo, 525 Washington St., Buffalo, NY 14203; (716) 856-4494.

Children's Aid Society, 150 E. 45th St., New York, NY 10017; (212) 949-4854.

North Carolina

State Agency: Division of Social Services, North Carolina Department of Human Resources, 325 N. Salisbury St., Raleigh, NC 27611; (919) 733-3801.

State Exchange: North Carolina Adoption Resource Exchange, same as above.

North Dakota

State Agency: Children and Family Services, North Dakota Department of Human Services, Bismarck, ND 58505; (701) 224-2316.
No State Exchange.

Ohio

State Agency: Ohio Department of Human Services, 30 E. Broad St., Columbus, OH 43266; (614) 466-8510.

State Exchange: Ohio Adoption Resource Exchange, same as above.

Oklahoma

State Agency: Oklahoma Department of Human Services, P.O. Box 25352, Oklahoma City, OK 73125; (405) 521-4373.

State Exchange: Oklahoma Children's Adoption Resource Exchange, P.O. Box 60934, Oklahoma City, OK 73146.

Oregon

State Agency: Adoption Services, Oregon Children's Services Division, 198 Commercial St. SE, Salem, OR 97310; (503) 378-4452.
No State Exchange.

Pennsylvania

State Agency: Pennsylvania Adoption Exchange, Lanco Lodge, Second Floor, P.O. Box 2675, Harrisburg, PA 17105-2675; (717) 257-7015.

State Exchange: same as above.

Rhode Island

State Agency: Rhode Island Department for Children and Their Families, 610 Mt. Pleasant Ave., Providence, RI 029008; (401) 457-4545.
State Exchange: Ocean State Adoption Resource Exchange, 500 Prospect St., Pawtucket, RI 02860; (401) 724-1910.

South Carolina

State Agency: South Carolina Department of Social Services, Adoption Unit, P.O. Box 1520, Columbia, SC 29202; (803) 734-6112.
State Exchange: South Carolina Seedlings, Route 13, Box 298, Easley, SC 29640; (803) 269-7713.

South Dakota

State Agency: Child Protection Services, South Dakota Department of Social Services, 700 Governors Dr., Pierre, SD 57501; (605) 773-3227.
No State Exchange.

Tennessee

State Agency: Tennessee Department of Human Services, Citizens Plaza Building, 400 Deaderick St., Nashville, TN 37219; (615) 741-5935.
State Exchange: Tennessee Adoption Resource Exchange, same as above.

Texas

State Agency: Texas Department of Human Resources, P.O. Box 2960, 706 Banister Ln., Austin, TX 78769; (512) 450-3357.
State Exchange: Texas Adoption Resource Exchange, same as above.

Vermont

State Agency: Vermont Social Services, 103 S. Main St., Waterbury, VT 05676; (802) 241-2150.

Virginia

State Agency: Commonwealth of Virginia, Department of Social Services, 8007 Discovery Dr., Richmond, VA 23288; (804) 281-9131.

State Exchange: Adoption Resource Exchange of Virginia, address same as above; (804) 281-9151.

Bethany Christian Services, 246 Maple Ave. E., Suite 200, Vienna, VA 22180; (703) 255-4775.

LDS Social Services, P.O. Box 638, 8110 Virginia Pine Ct., Chesterfield, VA 23832; (804) 743-0727.

Washington

State Agency: Washington Division of Children and Family Services, OB41-C, Olympia, WA 98504; (206) 753-0965.

State Exchange: Washington Adoption Resource Exchange, same as above.

Bethany Christian Services, 103 E. Holly, Suite 316, Bellingham, WA 98225; (206) 733-6042.

LDS Social Services Kennewick Office, 6500-B W. Bescheutes, Kennewick, WA 99336; (509) 735-8406.

LDS Social Services Seattle Office, 220 South Third Pl., Renton, WA 98055; (206) 624-3393.

LDS Social Services Spokane Office, N. 606 Pines Rd., Spokane, WA 99216; (509) 926-6581.

New Hope of Washington, 2611 NE 125th, Suite 146, Seattle, WA 98125; (206) 363-1800.

West Virginia

State Agency: West Virginia Department of Human Services, Child Welfare, 1900 Washington St., Charleston, WV 25305; (304) 348-7980.

State Exchange: West Virginia Adoption Exchange, P.O. Box 2942, Charleston, WV 25330; (304) 346-1062.

Wisconsin

State Agency: Wisconsin Department of Health and Social Services, Division of Community Services, Bureau for Children, Youth and

Families, 1 West Wilson St., P.O. Box 7851, Madison, WI 53707; (608) 266-0690.
State Exchange: Coalition for Children in Families, P.O. Box 10176, Milwaukee, WI 53210.
Bethany Christian Services, W255 N477 Grandview Blvd., Suite 207, Waukesha, WI 53188; (414) 547-6557.

Wyoming

State Agency: Wyoming Division of Public Assistance and Social Services, Hathaway Building, Cheyenne, WY 82002-0710; (307) 777-6891.

International Adoption Agencies

This list is by no means inclusive. More information may be available from state adoption exchanges and social services departments. *A Guide to International Adoption* (Willow Oak Press, P.O. Box 684, Long Valley, NJ 07853) also provides essential information.

- Child Welfare League of America, 67 Irving Place, New York, NY 10003; (212) 254-7410.
- Committee for Single Adoptive Parents, P.O. Box 15084, Chevy Chase, MD 20815.
- International Concerns Committee for Children, 911 Cypress Dr., Boulder, CO 80303; (303) 494-8333.
- North American Council for Adoptable Children, 1821 University Ave., Suite N-498, St. Paul, MN 55104; (612) 644-3036.

Among the international agencies listed in the 1989 *Adoption Factbook* by the National Committee for Adoption are these:

Australia

LDS Social Services, 33 Clarendon St., Suite 2, South Melbourne, Victoria 3205, Australia; 011-613-690-4344.

LDS Social Services, 15 Parnell St., 1st Floor, Suite 1, Strathfield, N.S.W.
2135, Australia; 011-612-747-5211.

Canada

LDS Social Services, 2 Dunbloor Rd., Suite 304, Islington, Ontario,
Canada M9A 2E4; (416) 542-2470.
LDS Social Services Calgary Office, 7040 Farrell Rd. SE, Calgary,
Alberta, Canada T2H OT2.
LDS Social Services Lethbridge Office, Box SS 1-1-34, Lethbridge,
Alberta, Canada T1J 4B3; (403) 328-8263.

England

LDS Social Services, 399 Garretts Green Ln., Sheldon, Birmingham
B33 OUH, England; 011-44-21-784-9266.

New Zealand

LDS Social Services, P.O. Box 33-848, Takapuna, Auckland 9, New
Zealand; 011-64-9497-158.

Romania

More than 100,000 children (ages infant to eighteen years old)
remain in Romania's institutions. In the early 1990s, hopeful American parents viewed Romania and its orphanages as the place to go
overseas in seeking an adoptive child.

Abuses of the system caused the Romanian government to close
off adoptions. But a new Romanian law, the "Abandonment Law,"
enacted in July, 1993, has begun to change that situation, allowing
adoption by foreign parents willing to travel to Romania and spend
an estimated $20,000.

As in all foreign adoptions, it is always best for prospective
parents to contact the American Immigration and Naturalization
Service for updated information on foreign adoption. The INS also
prepares a helpful booklet, *The Immigration of Adopted and Prospective Adoptive Children.* You can receive a copy by writing to

the service at 425 I Street, Washington, DC 20536. For more information, contact the INS district offices in your state, or contact the United States Department of State at (202) 647-3444.

Those seeking a Romanian child must know that some "private" adoptions are allowed. Not all children in orphanages are considered officially abandoned. Thousands, however, meet the criteria of being abandoned after they have had no parental "interest" for six months. These children are available only through a few government-approved adoption agencies. In Romania only six of the thousands of adoption agencies dealing with international adoptions have been approved to operate:

Bethany Christian Services, 901 Eastern Ave., NE, Grand Rapids, MI
    49503-1295.
Holt International, P.O. Box 2880, Eugene, OR 97402.
Life Adoption Services, Inc., 440 W. Main St., Tustin, CA 92680.
Small World Ministries, 401 Bonnaspring Dr., Hermitage, TN 37076.
WACAP, P.O. Box 88948, Seattle, WA 98138.
Welcome House Adoption Services, P.O. Box 18901, Doylestown, PA
    18901.

For further information on Romanian children and their plight, parents may also write to the Brooke Foundation, 1070 Race Street, Unit C, Denver, CO 80206. The foundation operates ROSES (Romanian Orphans Social Educational Services Project).

GLOSSARY

To assist your understanding, we define the terms common to the social services and adoption fields that are used in the book.

AIDS: Acquired immune deficiency syndrome, which is fatal and has no cure.

Adoption: The matching of a child to a family that can love, guide and understand him. A lifelong attachment and commitment is the desired result.

Apgar score: Developed by Dr. Virginia Apgar to rate babies' conditions after labor and delivery. Her test awards the baby 0, 1 or 2 points on each of five newborn characteristics (color, respiratory effort, heart rate, muscle tone and reflux irritability). A score of 7–10 points is considered good. The test is given one minute and again five minutes after birth.

Apnea: The inability to regulate breathing. Sleep apnea occurs when a person temporarily stops breathing during sleep. Apnea has been linked to sudden infant death syndrome (SIDS).

Artificial insemination: Impregnation of a woman by injecting sperm by artificial means.

Attachment: "Attachment" and "bonding" are similar terms, although many experts believe bonding is what happens during the first few minutes after birth when a baby is held by its mother. Attachment happens during the first eighteen months of life, when an infant experiences a need (pain, hunger or discomfort), expresses it and has it gratified by the primary care giver (usually the mother). As this cycle is repeated thousands of times during this early period of life, a strong trust bond develops between the child and the care giver. It is this cycle of trust that enables a child to later accept limits and controls. Any interruption of the cycle is called a "break."

Birth parents: Alternately known as "natural" or "genetic" parents. The individuals who gave life to the child.

Boarder babies: Infants left in maternity wards by their parents, often because they are born drug-addicted or HIV-positive. These infants remain in the hospital long after there is a medical reason for them to be there.

Bonding: See Attachment.

Challenged: Living with mental, physical or emotional disabilities.

Chlamydia: A sexually transmitted disease that can blind or impair the eyesight of babies.

Congregate care: Another term for group homes, residential treatment facilities and orphanages.

Dizygotic: Fraternal twins who do not have the same genetic makeup because they develop from different eggs.

Dysfunctional: Not functioning in a healthy manner. Generally this refers to families that are incompetent or unable to care for their children's emotional and/or physical needs. One example is parents who are drug-addicted.

Fetal alcohol effect (FAE): A birth condition connected to excessive use of alcohol during pregnancy that may cause disabilities.

Fetal alcohol syndrome (FAS): More serious than FAE, this is a birth defect that can cause facial deformities, including small eyes; an undersize head; a long, flat upper lip; predisposition to learning disabilities; a short attention span and hyperactivity.

Fos/Adopt: A parenting situation in which foster parents are given first priority to adopt a child placed in their home. Generally, the foster parents are paid a stipend to care for the child. Sometimes a small payment continues after adoption. Also known as "adoptive foster care."

Foster care: A way to provide a safe, secure home for foundling children. The U.S. foster care system evolved from the orphanage system around the turn of the century. Foster care parents receive a stipend to pay for the child's expenses, such as food and clothing, although it is often grossly inadequate.

Fragile genetics: A child who is born into a dysfunctional family and may carry a predisposition for mental illness, alcoholism and drug dependency.

Free for adoption: A child legally released by birth parents.

Gamete intra-Fallopian transfer (GIFT): A fertilization procedure in which a physician injects eggs and sperm into the female's Fallopian tubes. This cutting-edge procedure is costly and, because it can result in multiple births, is rarely used.

Genetics: The order arranged in the DNA of the molecules that transmit genetic information to the cells in a corresponding order, dictating the heredity with which each individual is born. There is increasing scientific evidence that each person inherits certain characteristics and temperaments that affect that individual for life. For example, evidence mounts that such challenges as alcoholism are genetically transmitted to offspring.

Group home: A family that takes in a number of foster children, usually less than ten, and cares for them as if they were members of a large family. Children assigned to group homes often are very difficult and may have psychological problems.

Heritability: Like genetics, heritability refers to the likelihood that certain traits will be inherited through a family bloodline and passed to a later generation.

High risk: Pertains to children with prenatal or birth complications; who are born with physical or mental challenges, or to parents with little education, chronic illness, psychiatric problems or substance abuse problems; who may be raised in poverty, abused or neglected.

HIV-positive: Infected with HIV, the virus that causes AIDS.

Infertility: The inability to have a child. It can be caused by certain contraceptive devices, including the Dalkon Shield; by sexually transmitted diseases; by advancing age (the biological clock has run out) or by defective genes.

Intrafamilial: Within a family, as in adoption by relatives. Often it means adoption by the new marriage partner of the birth parent, or by the genetic grandparents.

In vitro fertilization: One of the technologies used to help infertile couples conceive. Eggs from the woman and sperm from the man are joined outside of the woman's body, then placed into the woman's womb to attach and grow.

Monozygotic: Identical twins, who share the same genetic makeup because they come from the same egg.

Nature: The genetic/organic heritage a child carries.

Nurture: The environmental factors at work while children grow. The term usually refers to any influence on the child from outside sources.

Permanency plan: A plan set up by social services that ensures a child can move through the adoption process to a permanent home as soon as possible, spending not more than several months in a protective foster care situation before adoption.

PWBS: Perfect white babies.

Reflux: The tendency for food to roll back up the esophagus, sometimes causing scar tissue and vomiting. This condition is often caused by prenatal exposure to drugs.

Residential treatment: In-patient institutions that provide treatment and therapy to children with psychological problems. Children assigned to them typically can not make it in a family situation, often because they have had multiple adoption/foster care placements. Cost of residential treatment is skyrocketing.

Resilience: The ability to achieve emotional health and competence in spite of severe or prolonged adversity or stress.

SIDS: Sudden infant death syndrome. The unexplained death of an infant. Sometimes associated with apnea.

Special needs: Children labeled as "special needs" include these categories: children over age five; sibling groups; children of color; children with psychological, developmental or physical challenges (including crack, HIV and AIDS babies).

STD: Sexually transmitted disease.

Surrogate: A woman who carries another's child by contract. She is impregnated by artificial insemination or embryo implant.

Temperament: The preferred name for a variety of initial, inherited traits.

Utero: As used in this volume, utero refers to the fetus while in the womb. Any interruption of the fetus' development is considered to be *in utero*, including the use of certain drugs, such as cocaine, which can severely interrupt the development of a fetus.

BIBLIOGRAPHY

There are many books that can be helpful with various problems or issues of adoption. A suggested reading list:

Arms, Suzanne. *Adoption: A Handful of Hope*. Berkeley, CA: Celestial Arts, 1990.

———. *To Love and Let Go*. New York: Alfred Knopf, 1983.

Brodzinsky, Anne Braff. *The Mulberry Bird: Story of an Adoption*. Indianapolis: Perspectives Press, 1986.

Caplan, Lincoln. *An Open Adoption*. New York: Farrar, Straus & Giroux, 1990.

Cline, Foster, M.D. *Hope for High Risk and Rage-Filled Children*. Evergreen, CO: EC Publications, 1992.

Dorris, Michael. *The Broken Cord: A Family's Ongoing Struggle with Fetal Alcohol Syndrome*. New York: Harper & Row, 1989.

Dunn, Linda Ed. *Adopting Children with Special Needs: A Sequel*. Washington, DC: North American Council on Adoptable Children, 1983.

Freudberg, Judy, and Tony Geiss. *Susan and Gordon Adopt a Baby*. New York: Random House, 1986.

Gabel, Susan. *Filling in the Blanks: A Guided Look at Growing Up Adopted*. Indianapolis: Perspectives Press, 1988.

Gilman, Lois. *The Adoption Resource Book*. New York: Harper & Row, 1984.

Irwin, Hadley. *Kim/Kimi*. New York: Margaret K. McElderry Books, 1987.

Jewett, Claudia. *Helping Children Cope with Separation and Loss*. Harvard Common Press, 1982.

Johnston, Patricia. *An Adopter's Advocate*. Indianapolis: Perspectives Press, 1984.

————. *Understanding: A Guide to Impaired Fertility for Family and Friends*. Indianapolis: Perspectives Press, 1983.

Koch, Janice. *Our Baby: A Birth and Adoption Story*. Indianapolis: Perspectives Press, 1985.

Krementz, Jill. *How It Feels to Be Adopted*. New York: Alfred Knopf, 1982.

Lindsay, Jeanne Warren. *Open Adoption: A Caring Option*. Buena Park, CA: Morning Glory Press, 1988.

Livingston, Carole. *Why Was I Adopted?* Secaucus, NJ: Lyle Stuart, 1978.

Magnusen, Debbe. *It's Never Dull*. Great Bend, KS: C.E.D.A.R. & DeDay Publishing, 1991.

McHugh, Elisabeth. *Karen's Sister*. New York: Greenwillow Books, 1983.

McKelvey, Carole, and Ken Magid. *High Risk: Children without a Conscience*. New York: Bantam Books, 1988.

Melina, Lois. *Making Sense of Adoption: A Parent's Guide*. New York: Harper & Row, 1989.

Menning, Barbara. *Infertility: A Guide for the Childless Couple*. Englewood Cliffs, NJ: Prentice Hall, 1977.

Michelman, Stanley B., et al. *The Private Adoption Handbook: A Step-by-Step Guide to the Legal, Emotional, and Practical Demands of Adopting a Baby*. Dell Books, 1988.

National Committee for Adoption. *Adoption Factbook, 1989*. Washington, DC: National Committee for Adoption, 1988.

Plumez, Jacqueline Hornor. *Successful Adoption: A Guide to Finding a Child and Raising a Family*. New York: Harmony Books, 1987.

Powledge, Fred. *So You're Adopted*. New York: Charles Scribner's Sons, 1982.

Schaffer, Patricia. *How Babies and Family Are Made—There Is More Than One Way!* Berkeley, CA: Tabor Sarah Books, 1988.

Smith, Jerome, and Franklin Miroff. *You're Our Child: The Adoption Experience.* Lanham, MD: University Press of America, 1981.

Sorosky, A. D., Annette Baran, and Reyben Pannor. *The Adoption Triangle: The Effects of the Sealed Record on Adoptees, Birth Parents and Adoptive Parents.* New York: Anchor Press/ Doubleday, 1984.

Welch, Martha, M.D. *Holding Time.* New York: Simon & Schuster, 1988.

INDEX

A

Abortion, 30–31

Abuse, 26, 33, 37, 38, 41–42, 45, 48, 60, 65, 66, 67, 68, 69, 70, 73, 74, 77, 78, 79, 82, 83, 84–85, 87, 104, 119

Acquired immune deficiency syndrome (AIDS), 8, 98–100

Adopted child syndrome, 137

Adoption counseling (pre- and post-), 60, 70, 87, 141, 178

Adoption and Disruption: Rates, Risks and Responses, 49

Adoption Factbook, 71, 106, 118

Adoption fees, 52–53, 149

Adoption subsidies, 87

Adoption Worker's Guide to Genetic Services, 134

Adoptions of Yugoslav children, 113

Agencies, 59–60

Alcohol-exposed babies, 39, 40

Alcoholism, 37, 89, 100, 104, 127, 128, 129–31

American Psychological Association, 140

American Psychologist, 140

Apnea, 90, 101

Artificial insemination, 21

Attachment Center at Evergreen, 68, 80, 84, 132

F

G

H

I